SEASONS OF THE SPIRIT

Exploring Contemporary Spirituality

Clyde F. Crews

A Liturgical Press Book

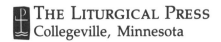

THE LITURGICAL PRESS
Collegeville, Minnesota

Excerpts from W. H. Auden in *W. H. Auden: Collected Poems* edited by Edward Mendelson are reprinted by permission of Random House, Inc., © 1976.

Excerpts from *Mass* by Leonard Bernstein and Stephen Schwartz are reprinted by permission of Amberson Inc. and Stephen Schwartz and Jalmi Publication, Inc., publishers; and Boosey and Hawkes, agents, © 1971.

Excerpts from E. E. Cummings in *e. e. cummings: Poems 1923–1954* are reprinted by permission of Liveright Publishing Corporation, © 1968.

Excerpts from Gerard Manley Hopkins in *The Poems of G. M. Hopkins* edited by W. H. Gardner, © 1967; from Percy Bysshe Shelley in *The Complete Poetical Works of Percy Bysshe Shelley*, edited by T. Hutchinson, © 1960; and from William Wordsworth in *The Poetical Works of William Wordsworth*, edited by T. Hutchinson, © 1965, are reprinted by permission of Oxford University Press.

Excerpts from Theodore Roethke in *Collected Poems of Theodore Roethke*, © 1966 are reprinted by permission of Doubleday, a division of Bantam, Dell Publishing Group, Inc.

Excerpts from D. H. Lawrence in *The Complete Poems of D. H. Lawrence*, edited by Vivian de Sola Pinto and Warren Roberts, © 1964, are reprinted by permission of Penguin U.S.A.

All biblical references are from the Jerusalem Bible except those otherwise specifically noted:

NAV— New American Version of Sacred Scripture made by members of the Catholic Biblical Association and as used in *Lectionary for the Mass*.
NRSV—New Revised Standard Version

Cover design by Ann L. Blattner
Cover photograph by Clyde F. Crews

1   2   3   4   5   6   7   8   9

Library of Congress Cataloging-in-Publication Data

Crews, Clyde F.
  Seasons of the spirit : exploring contemporary spirituality /
Clyde F. Crews.
     p.   cm.
  Includes bibliographical references.
  ISBN 0-8146-2081-7
  1. Church year meditations. 2. Spiritual life—Catholic authors.
I. Title.
BX2170.C55C74 1992
242'.3—dc 20   92-24115
                                                            CIP

For Clara
1921–1987

May she rest—and revel—in peace

CONTENTS

SECTION THREE: PRAYERS

INTRODUCTION

Our lives are an alphabet that the Spirit spells. Our days are the words; our weeks the paragraphs; our months and years the chapters and volumes. As we write our unique stories, a tale of the blending of divine and human energies, we probe over and again the great mysteries hidden deep within us all. And for those of us who are Christian in our call, there is a deep grammar with which to structure our understanding of the self, the community, the earth and the Ultimate. That grammar is none other than the mysteries of faith as proclaimed and enacted in the cycle of seasons that constitute the Christian year.

By attending closely, carefully, to the great liturgical seasons, we see and hear again the great story of God and humanity. And we do more. We enter into such a cycle, turning from isolation and entering profoundly into connectedness with that which is primal, enlivening, lasting.

Primitives and moderns alike have sought to plunge into the eternal through rituals of sacred time and sacred space, according to the landmark studies of the late historian of religions, Mircea Eliade. These unnumbered millions have longed to join their lone stories to the great human narrative, not in order to lose their selves, but precisely in order to discover them more truly.

Christians, blessed with a more penetrating insight into the dignity and destiny of the human, thus join their efforts to the vast multitudes of the earth—those many recorded by history and those more numerous who have left no traces. In entering into such a chorus, Christians take part in a more extensive "communion of saints" than even they may have at first realized. In doing so, they learn to integrate into their lives struggle and peace; pain and joy; the individual and the community; the temporal and the eternal.

Accordingly, the first section of these pages turns to reflections upon many of the great feasts and seasons of the Christian heart: Advent, Christmas, Lent, Easter, Pentecost, Assumption, and All Saints. It attempts to explore the intensity with which such days can speak to our contemporary experience, bringing balance, compassion, and meaning to an era of exaggeration, competition, violence, and the shaking of old foundations. These holy seasons can invite the living of more truly human lives.

But the achievement of community and connection brings more than stability and satisfaction. Those who are blessed are bid to become themselves blessings for others. Faith gives birth not only to inner feelings of contentment, but to imperatives of action and service as well.

The precise statement of mandates of faith are legion in the literature of Jewish and Christian faith. In Micah 6:8, for example, believers are bid "to act justly, to love tenderly, and to walk humbly with God." The readers and hearers of Paul receive all manner of direct exhortation. Consider Colossians 3:15-16: "Always be thankful. Let the message of Christ in all its richness find a home with you." Jesus himself could be surpassingly direct in his imperative voice as well. To the Pharisees in Matthew 9:13 he addresses the withering command: "Go and learn the meaning of the words: What I want is mercy and not sacrifice."

Thus the second section of these essays will make so bold as to probe many of the implications for discipleship in the modern world, as well as the ancient infinitives of the heart: to search for authenticity; to bring challenge and comfort to society; to touch the scars; to cast out fear; to make the Spirit visible; to transform and to be transformed; to lift up hearts; to go home to the Kingdom of God. Each of these missions of the Christian heart continually intersects, illuminates, and enriches the others.

The collection ends with a brief third section composed of morning and evening prayers. These are not meant as a pious flourish with which to conclude. Rather they attempt to gather up themes from throughout the collection, and bring them forward as elements of the life of prayer. Many "borrowings" from great masters and mistresses of spiritual life dot these matins and vespers lines. They have gone forward into the fuller life of God. I trust they will not mind if I do not footnote them.

-cfc-

Section One
HOLY SEASONS

A STREETCAR NAMED CHRISTMAS
An Advent Reflection

John the Baptist was probably as close as the first century came to producing an up-front rock video star look-alike. If we go just by the biblical descriptions we have of him, we wouldn't be far off in naming him a candidate for MTV. The way he dressed . . . the things he ate . . . the way he acted were all . . . to put a word on it, a little unusual, not to say eccentric. He was fully in the tradition of the prophet.

John said little that got recorded. MTV people usually don't make it to Nightline. Yet, a certain one-liner of this forerunner of Jesus, recorded in the Gospel of John, proves to be as insightful and eloquent as a Nobel Prize address. "There is one among you," John said, "whom you do not recognize" (John 1:26) NAV.

Wrapped up in ten English words. There is the meaning of Advent. There is the substance of the Christian call in its clearest, bluntest, and starkest form: There is one among you whom you do not recognize.

Advent is in truth about something we do every day of our lives: waiting. We wait for a bus. Or for grades to come in the mail. We wait for better health or greater happiness. We wait for death or we wait for a fuller life. Waiting is part of the dynamic of our lives

> because we are never complete;
>
> because we are all of us puzzles with new pieces always showing up;
>
> because patience is one of our most important gifts and products.

We work while we wait, but we are waiters all the same. And are meant to be.

The prophet sometimes called Tritero-Isaiah (the third major literary hand, most likely, in the creation of the Book of Isaiah) certainly offers a vision of a life worth working for. Worth waiting for. His people—like all people at one time or another—have seen things approaching their worst. They had known want, indignity, depression, and desolation. But as their exile draws to an end, they catch a glimpse of a newer, more integrated vision of things in which such harsh realities as they have known are perceived as part of a more complete and intricate script.

There had been darkness. But that very darkness has underscored both the need for and the undying reality of light. And the light, as it must, began to break through (Isaiah 61).

The prophet Isaiah describes the new day already arriving on the calendar of the heart. It is a day of rejoicing but also a day with work to be done:

> the bringing of elation and hope in the midst of shadows and grumblings;
>
> the healing and cheering of bruised and broken hearts;
>
> the freeing or at least improving of those caught in the webs and captivities of life;
>
> the making more palpably present the ongoing presence of God in our midst.

This stunning passage from Isaiah was the very one read by the young Jesus in the synagogue at Nazareth as reported in Luke 4:18. It was a wonderfully dramatic moment. The young man read the scroll. And every eye was fixed on him, the text says. Today, he assures them, this text is in the process of fulfillment.

He was telling them that what they were awaiting was already in their midst. And always would be. Their job was to recognize it for what it was, to travel toward it and within it, to make it their own.

Isn't that, too, the message of Advent? To call each of us to that which should be obvious, yet isn't? Maybe some of us do not recognize what and who is among us in thousands of ways and places and events. Maybe we are waiting for the wrong emotional bus, for the wrong metaphysical trolley. Maybe the one we so desperately need is the very one we're avoiding time after time.

Advent can be a chart leading us on the right transportation line, the right track. We say, each of us, that Christmas is some kind of destination. We know for a fact that it exerts an enormous emotional hold on people of all ages. But if Christmas is meant to celebrate only complete physical satisfaction, or sentimentality, or having everything just our own way in life, we're in for surprise and more than surprise. We're in for disappointment.

Rather, Christmas has other lessons to teach. Lessons that are the gladdest of tidings—if we know how to listen. Lessons that will start to heal our brokenness—if we know how to respond. Lessons that can start to free us from our frequent sense of futility—if we know how to act and believe.

Christmas teaches us:

> about the triumph of ordinary things well done, even when we don't want to do them;
>
> about our need to become childlike in our trust but parental and adult in our responsibilities;
>
> about our need to live patiently with the imperfections in ourselves and with the unexpected around ourselves;
>
> that we have been freed from the awful responsibility of having to grasp at life's meaning or the desperation of having to force our own purposes upon it;
>
> that meaning is already in our midst if we are patient and listen and learn. We don't need to grab for eternity. It has sought us out. Cradled us and called us by name. Has told us to live our little lives well.

The disciples of Jesus at last caught on to these promises and possibilities. They saw something in him that made all the difference in their lives. They saw it after not having seen it for a long time, even when they were with him. There was one among them whom they did not recognize.

Dominican theologian Edward Schillebeeckx writes: "Suddenly they saw it. He [and all that he stood for] was the guarantee of the renewal of *their* lives." The birth of Jesus is also about *our* coming to birth. His nativity, our nativity. His Christmas, our Christmas. But first we have to get there. To Christmas.

We won't get there at all if we take the wrong way. If we take the streetcar named "Perfection in All Things" we won't make it. Nor if it is marked "Total Control of My Life" or "Self-Satisfaction on My Terms" or "Rank Dishonesty" or "Infidelity" or "Manipulation" or "Promiscuity" or a thousand other names of items available on the modern moral smorgasbord.

No, if we want to reach a wholeness and honesty of life, we have to take the streetcar named Inner Christmas. Short of that, we'll never come to that Second Birth we all so eagerly desire, whether we know it or not. Consider the wonderful words of the old Christmas carol "Hark the Herald Angels Sing" written in 1739 by Wesley:

> Mild he lays his glory by
> Born that man no more may die
> Born to raise the sons of earth
> Born to give them second birth.

The way to the second birth for each of us is the way to our own inner nativity. There is a fare to be paid to reach such a state. It involves discipline and prayer, listening and service. It means that we are summoned to be patron saints of the possible:

> to make a difference, not in some imaginary tomorrow of perfection, but in the confusion of the now;

> to live out of our brokenness and to work toward healing;

> to make of our lives an invitation for others to live more fully and more freely;

> to see and encourage in others what they often do not recognize as strengths in themselves;

> to have a care for the mysteries, the troubles, even the darknesses in others, knowing that in some cases they may have travelled distances that we have not had to go.

Paul says in Thessalonians, one of the oldest of the New Testament writings: Rejoice always. It is a crazy thought to be sure as long as we persist in seeing things in an unspiritual perspective. If we insist that all there is to life is what we see and hear and have, then rejoicings will be few and far between, and not very lasting when they come. Streetcars going that direction do not end up at Christmas. They are streetcars named Futility.

> And so we wait. As we must.
> But we must wait well.
> For the streetcar named Christmas.
> And pray for the courage to board it.

A CRIB TOO SMALL
Thoughts at Christmas

Some years ago, a theology book appeared with a startling title: *Your God Is Too Small.* Its thesis was that all of us cling to an image of God too narrow to suggest the might and mercy of the true God. The time may have come for a seasonal sequel to that book, just in time for Christmas giving. Call it: *Your Crib Is Too Small.*

Your usual Christmas crib comes equipped with seven folks— Mary, Joseph, Baby Jesus, three Kings, and one Shepherd—also one angel, assorted camels, sheep, and if you're an upscale family, perhaps some oxen, too. You'll also find as standard issue three gifts—gold, frankincense, and myrrh. But if you attend to the liturgical readings of the week before Christmas, you'll find that the Church peoples our Christmas season with an amazing array of characters.

There we find the gentle Elizabeth, "filled with the Holy Spirit"; and Hannah, she of the revolutionary vision of a truly just society. The lovers of the Song of Songs show up, reminding us of how precious and exhilarating our love for others can be; how deeply it can carry us into the divine love itself. But others are invoked as well: Samson, the original macho man, whom one of our best Scripture scholars describes as a "murderous bandit"; and Samuel, Hannah's son, a seer, a man of visions, but also a revengeful warrior; and David, king and poet, who also doubles as a lusty, turbulent man of battle. An odd assortment, this.

But this is the scene, as one of our carols reminds us, where the hopes and fears of all the years are met. This is a privileged place, not just a sentimental one, where all people metaphysically gather, carrying within them all the scars and sins, all the nobility and graciousness of which humankind is capable. We all stand around that crib, gazing in awe at what Auden called "the uncontrollable mystery on the bestial floor." Rapt in wonder at the Child of Promise.

For that child carries within himself the secret and mystery of all of our lives. He is the emblem and the promise of all that we could hope or imagine for our lives, for those we hold dear, and for the troubled earth as it whirls through space. What we celebrate at Christmas is not his birth alone, but the possibility of new birth and new life for us all. His nativity is not his alone. His nativity can be our nativity as well.

But let us not stray too far from our best-seller . . . *Your Crib Is Too Small*. We have added some statues to the scene, but what about the gifts? What is Christmas without gifts? Surely the three at the traditional crib aren't enough. For the child, you see, is the giver of the very gifts that his visitors bring. The liturgical readings of this season bring us a priceless array of gifts—images and insights for our lives:

The Casting Out of Fear.

The Diminishment of Our Anxieties.

Light Overcoming the Darkness.

Spring Overtaking the Winter.

Swords Being Turned to Plowshares.

Justice in Society: mentioned not once, but at least half a dozen times in the week of Christmas.

Patience: even when it is sorely tried.

Inner Peace: no matter what life may bring to our path.

Endless Equanimity: even amidst our troubles.

Strength: even though our weaknesses do not vanish.

Wisdom: even though we stumble through our often confused days.

Whether we have the usual small crib, or the new improved and expanded model, it only serves our Christmas purpose if we use it aright. Only if we realize that when we gaze at it, we look not only at the Babe, but also at the person he calls us to become. We are all and always children, able to learn, to change, to start again. Christmas always tugs at our heartstrings because it assures us, even in a secular, sometimes cynical age, that the things we long for—as well as our sweetest memories and deepest imaginings—are not illusion, but reality.

Death is not our destiny. Nativity is.

All because of the little one there that Scripture is pleased to call the *Dayspring*. The light beginning to break the darkness. We too must begin to shine in the darkness . . . put off grumpiness and self-absorption; begin to put on the swaddling clothes of joy and the reaching out to others that ends in the reward of a grander and fuller self.

Christmas and its crib are not escape from reality; they are a plunging into it. Among the traditional gifts the kings bring is myrrh, a burial spice. The crib is the first step to the Cross. Both are made of the self-same wood. But both Christmas and the Cross lead beyond, to more than the obvious or the imaginable. We base our lives on that. That, too, is part of the deep mystery and majesty of this feast.

We must not leave these ruminations on the crib without a reference to that critter who stands atop it: the angel. In the cinema of our own time, in the German film *Wings of Desire,* we find a powerfully renewed image of what "angel" might mean: a presence that wraps us round and caresses us to give us strength in our need. The angel, too, gives us a signal of what our lives might be. The angels, G. K. Chesterton said, could fly precisely because they took themselves so lightly.

We can take ourselves lightly, too. Don't have to have those awful draining drives . . . ego compulsions . . . grasping desires. We must share and serve and care and change—but without anxiety or drudgery or glumness. We are not alone. The God of the Ages, the Child of Christmas, is our constant companion. We can soar. We can frolic. We can take ourselves lightly, for God takes us seriously, each and every one.

RISK AND RADIANCE
A Lenten Reflection

Then Jesus told his disciples, "If any want to become my followers, let them deny themselves and take up their cross and follow me. For those who want to save their life will lose it, and those who lose their life for my sake will find it. For what will it profit them if they gain the whole world but forfeit their life? (Matt 16:24-26) NRSV.

"King Christ this world is all aleak:
and life-preservers there are none."

So wrote E. E. Cummings in a poem titled "No Thanks."

And he seems to speak for all of us, at least on given days, or in given periods of our lives. There are just times when we sense that things are coming undone around us: our bodies, perhaps; or our plans, friendships, projects, happiness, meaning, our very life itself. Death becomes something of a final symbol, symptom, and reality of our state. We feel adrift, and life preservers there are none.

The older most of us get, the more we become convinced of the wisdom of the scientific perception of entropy. All matter of its nature tends to become scattered, sliding irresistibly downward, so that eventually, at some point in time, there will be no energy left to use; all activity will have stopped; all that would be left would be atoms in the stellar vacuum. But we don't need scientific analysis to tell us about entropy. We've all felt it—at seven in the morning or five in the evening—or at other times of the day; a sense of drain and futility.

21

What have such dismal considerations to do with the Christian observance of Lent, with the preparation for a celebration of Easter? In a way they have everything to do with such a holy season. For Lent is Christianity's Yom Kippur, its time of critical self-scrutiny; its invitation to reflection, awareness of limitation, change, choice, and risk.

Just as Advent-Christmas is a cycle celebrating the incarnation, and summons us to patience and expectancy, so Lent-Easter represents the other great pole of Christian faith—the assertion of action and transformation under the power of grace. Lent speaks of process, painful birth, the casting out of a legion of unholy attitudes and loves so that the Spirit of Christ risen and triumphant over all death and diminishment may truly be in some way one with our own spirits.

Lent is the time both of our contradiction and our consolation. The false self must be contradicted; and to that false self each of us in our own particular way so desperately clings. This may mean the contradicting of some of our most insistently selfish drives. As Stanley Hauerwas noted in *Vision and Virtue,* ''We have impoverished our ethics by assuming that our lives can easily embody and reflect the good.'' Passion Week, which climaxes the whole Lenten season, surely teaches us the frightful cost of virtue and Christic goodness. But Easter insists as well how worthy is the price of such graced effort.

So we must also speak of the consolation of such a season. There exists, in fact, for us a realistic hope that even in our brokenness and scars and sins, there is a Lord who has gone before us into the terrible darkness and now stands with us, while beckoning to us from beyond. That Lord Jesus whom we remember and treasure and join more intimately in this holy time is the very Lord who insists that a divine energy outdistances all entropy and that even the most bitter personal winter can turn at last to spring.

The Resurrection of this Christ Jesus, Christianity has insisted from its inception, speaks not only about the Lord, but about all people of all times and places without exception. As Monika Hellwig has phrased it: ''The resurrection of Jesus . . . is a sign of the compassionate power of the Father . . . which guarantees the meaning and purpose not only of the life and death of Jesus but of all human life and death.''

Lent signals to us that we must begin to abandon many of our false securities and to trust God and believe in that "highest human destiny and godlike seed which has been sown within" the human heart *(Gaudium et Spes)*. Lent involves the risk of a fundamental recasting of our vision, attitudes, and approaches to the world. It means that we chance losing old familiarities, even losing something of the old self. After all, if we are content in this life only to leave it as we find it, we may well lose it. That is the searing insight of Jesus who cautions us at the same time about gaining a world of illusion while losing a kingdom of unsearchable peace, both here and hereafter.

These forty days provide each of us a personal agenda of choice, insecurities, and risks. We too can take up a cross and be transformed by it. We may find this difficult to believe because we so often shortchange the imagination and the goodness of God.

For each of us there is the desert, the forty days—a time:

> to return to a questioning of the purpose and quality of our days;
>
> to choose direction over drift and futility;
>
> to be on guard against those diminishments that make of life itself a living death.

This time should be for all of us a positive time, but a time of casting out the false urgencies and intensities that devil our days and obscure for us the light of life to which we are called. We may need to cast behind us suppressed and misplaced angers, or superficialities, or infidelities or sloth or prayerlessness . . . debilitating fears or morose introspections.

Whatever our greatest personal need may be, Lent invites each of us to *begin* to change by *wanting* to change: by *praying* to change; by *working* to change. This is the privileged time in which to risk the moral journey of conversion away from the classical seven deadly sins:

> From *PRIDE* . . . to . . . *REALISM*
> We need in all candor to admit both our strengths and our weaknesses. False humility is as deadly as false pride. Abraham Maslow, for instance, speaks of the "Jonah Syndrome" —the evasion of one's growth, the deliberate setting of low

levels of aspiration . . . the refusal to make the attempt to
bear the superlative. The opposite extreme we might call the
Atlas Complex . . . that all the world depends upon ourselves alone.

From *ENVY* . . . to . . . *ENCOURAGEMENT*
So often when we begrudge others the gifts that they pos-
sess, it usually bespeaks a blindness to those with which we
are ourselves gifted. We can exert enormous energies waste-
fully in trying to become that which we have neither the call
nor capacity to become.

From *MISPLACED ANGER* . . . to . . . *EFFEC-
TIVENESS*
Anger can be a seething corrosive inside the self. It may be
inevitable, but it needs to be channelled. How easy it is for
us to churn all day over someone's tone of voice to us and
fail to become even slightly angered over hunger, indignity,
injustice, extravagant armament, callousness to the plight of
the unborn and the elderly . . . all in a society for which
we are in part responsible.

From *SLOTH* . . . to . . . *ENERGY FOR THE GOOD*
Laziness is more than sleepiness . . . it is a scattering of our
energies . . . a failure of our imagination, of creativity, of
the setting of priorities.

From *GREED* . . . to . . . *SHARING*
It is one of the oldest of human tricks to try to use the ac-
cumulation of things to establish our importance, our identity, our ultimate happiness. We need a minimum of things,
of course; but for full humanity and deep spirituality, we also
need some distance and some sharing.

From *GLUTTONY* . . . to . . . *CALM*
Gluttony speaks of a kind of restless agitation in the individual as well as a callousness in a culture that has to concen-
trate on dieting while one-third of the planet is malnourished.
We ferociously ingest, not only food, but also work and
projects as well . . . always filling our time with busyness
just as the glutton always restlessly fills the belly. God can,
after all, work in void and calm and quiet as well.

From *LUST* . . . to . . . *COMMITMENT AND RE-STRAINT*
It doesn't take a Puritan mind to admit that our age too often
sees sexuality only as a physical or pleasure function. It can
be a grace, a communication, a psychological experience of
immense power. And how often this society in its flight from
responsibility and commitment takes the erotic casually,
amusedly, functionally, cheaply, and without lifelong commitment.

We can't begin by undertaking all these conversions at once;
we must choose which will get our own personal priority. That
in itself is a kind of risk. And yet, we are called not just to ordinariness but to splendor. The stakes are high indeed.

Near the end of C. S. Lewis's fantasy *The Lion, The Witch and
the Wardrobe,* the Christ figure, the lion Aslan, has been resurrected
and sets to work breathing life upon the people turned to stone
by the power of evil. As each in turn comes at last to life, a riot
of holy and exhilarating vitality breaks forth. The ''magic deeper
still'' written indelibly in the universe and in each of our beings,
has worked. And as the Lion breathes life into each, one can only
recall Jesus who announced his task with arresting simplicity: I have
come so that they may have life and have it to the full (John 10:10).

Let the ashes of Lent then remind us of this mission and task:
we are called to come, at last, to life, in its complexity, its compassion, and its wit. We are summoned away from the engulfing waters
to the baptismal life. We are offered a life preserver of unspeakable
consequence. Will we reach for it? Will we be at last transubstantiated into the life that can be ours? In Lent, the Lord Jesus calls
us with special intensity and intimacy. Will we risk it? What is the
answer we shall give?

The late John Cheever spoke of our need to choose and to risk
in the great ventures of life. Reflecting on spirituality and virtue
in our morally murky age, Cheever said:

> One not only needs it, one struggles for it. It seems to me almost
> that one's total experience is the drive toward light.

Lent offers us a light just beginning to penetrate the darkness.
May we welcome it; nurture it; and let it rise to an Easter radiance.

THE SECURITY OF
THE CROSS
A Good Friday Meditation

Albert Camus, that thoughtful French Algerian who lacked the faith of Christians, remarked in *The Plague* that humanity shares three essentials in common: love, exile, and suffering. On Christianity's most somber day, Good Friday, as believers gather to venerate the Cross, they might reflect that in their observance, these three come strikingly together. The same Christ who bore the scars of pain, exile, and isolation, was also—to the utmost and to the end—the one who refused to dislodge love from its ultimate place in his perception of life.

The liturgy of this middle day of the great Triduum will speak eventually its consolation; but it first would have us know the sting and starkness of a warm-blooded life so shockingly undone. In that vulnerable figure upon the crucifix, what sensitive souls could fail to find images of their own fragility? We all spend time upon the cross.

The Cross is the most persistent symbol of Christian faith precisely because suffering is the least contestable fact of human existence. This intersected emblem of our mortality strikes at the human heart, shattering abstractions and easy consolations alike. If grief be not now in our personal midst, we know that some day it awaits us. We know full well that we are surrounded by a suffering humanity—often family and friends—for whom pain is all too current and insistent.

In truth, the Christian people come together on this night to reflect upon this mighty symbol of their personal and mutual affliction. They draw strength from such a solidarity in suffering. In being reminded of their common human condition, they are invited to compassion and reflection. They are called back from their trackless selfish wanderings to a geography of personal and communal authenticity.

But clearly, in such an observance, they seek to venerate more than reminders of their own vulnerabilities. For that they have not only their own experience, but *The New York Times,* NPR, CBS, and all the rest of it. The media all but shriek out at us that suffering erupts into peoples' lives, the just and the unjust, the kindly innocent and the bluntly guilty.

The minimalist, yet evocative, liturgy of Good Friday has much more to do than echo the daily news, or just solemnly render the latest exemplifications of humanity's ancient curse. Rather, this remembrance venerates and celebrates uncommonly more:

> a divine presence and stability in the midst of our suffering; and . . .

> a person, promise, and persistence at the very core of our lives.

That person is, of course, the friend and brother Jesus, truly divine and truly human. He was not the transitory visitor who was shown the prettier sights and then passed on. Rather was he like one who came to stay:

> to work and strain with us;
> to revel and sweat with us;
> to enter the blackest of our human nights.

The death of Jesus, that occurred under the direst of circumstances, testifies to the probity and commitment of his life. He could have loved less. He could have saved himself in an everyday sense. But he did not. He chose the more when the less would have done. Jesuit Karl Rahner has written of this Man of Sorrows in an essay titled "Following the Crucified":

> He was deprived of everything that is otherwise regarded as the content of a human existence: honor, life, acceptance in earthly and religious fellowship. In the concreteness of his life, it becomes only

too clear that everything fell away from him, even the perceptible security of the closeness of God's love. And in this trackless dark there prevailed silently only the mystery that in itself and in its freedom has no name and to which he nevertheless calmly surrendered himself as to eternal love, and not to the hell of futility. . . .

In this frightful crucible, in the maelstrom of events of the last hours of Jesus' life, we find the fuller dimension of the meaning of the Cross. It becomes the focal point not just of a death, but of a life lived without limit. For gathered into those days of the passion and death of Jesus is to be found the range of human depths and possibilities. It is evident in the tender farewell to friends; in the compassion for the women he meets on the way; in the forgiveness of tormentors. Through it all, he strives to act out the advice he gives the followers with which John begins the Last Supper Discourse: "Do not let your hearts be troubled" (John 14:1). Thus does he speak on the very eve of the Cross' dismal appearance. Thus does he announce to humanity the only genuine security on which the human heart can cast itself unreservedly.

Once Jesus has reached the supreme crisis, his own heart is sorrowful, but steadfast. He stands unflinchingly for the great values of trust, meaning and life, no matter how great the confusions around him; no matter what seeming securities fall away. Jesus stands when there is every reason to fall. Stands for life and its intensity and complexity, even in the face of the power of death. The divine love that he so uniquely embodies overcomes even that most ancient of enemies.

This is persistence in the primal meaning of the term. He does not demand complete explanations or insist upon some simple moral calculus. When tenderness seems in short supply or nonexistent, he *becomes* tenderness. When justice has been sent reeling, he *becomes* justice. When others scoff at his belief in all good things, he *becomes* trust. And when despair lurks about in every direction, he *becomes* hope. He brings to flesh-and-blood birth the great realities that we so often see only as hints and hunches. He incarnated the message of the 84th Psalm: that in passing through the bitter valley, the believer leaves behind a place of springs.

By his embracing of the Cross that Christendom so deeply venerates on Good Friday, Jesus not only offers us the very personification of endurance and courage, but of equanimity and promise as well. By entering so deeply into a death that is meant to affirm the great values of life, he gives life back to us . . . the only life worth having or living. A life incalculably finer than the lesser ones we have schemed for ourselves.

For those of us who stand under the power of that same Cross, who sign ourselves with its lines and meanings, the task of Jesus becomes our task; his promise, our promise. He now lives and calls us to live. Not the demi-life of our own imaginings. Not a clone life of his own terrestrial days. But a life uniquely our own, with himself as source of energy, imagination, constancy, and strength.

On this gravest of the Christian days of commemoration, believers ponder anew the inner crosses of their lives under the light and shading of the great primal Cross of Christ. And as we behold once again the arms outstretched of the compassionate Savior, we do well to hear with new force the words of a certain letter written to the early Church of Philippi so many centuries ago. Words that haunt us with their message; dizzy us with their implications; dazzle us with their simplicity. And the five words that enkindle us with new love, liberate us from our suffering, and call us home from exile are simply these:

Your attitude must be Christ's (Phil 2:6) NAV.

THE QUESTIONS OF EASTER

Once again, throughout most of the American landscape, the fields and grasslands have gone emerald green. Once again the yielding soil is turned over and the seeds of fruit, vegetable, and blossom are treasured up within. Once again in the "green cathedrals" of baseball parks, the crack of the bat is heard in the land. As the 1990s begin, in Eastern Europe, in Central America, in South Africa, spring has a new political and personal meaning; a significance that goes beyond season and climate and touches the very sinews of personal hope and collective imagination. And once again we find ourselves at another Passover and Easter of our lives.

These two primal feasts gladden both the Jewish and the Christian heart. They tell again the fundamental story of our lives. Remind us, for all the complexity that we manage to toss up around us, of the great simplicities of life. Both Easter and Passover tell us stories about ourselves that define and shape; that challenge and disturb; that tell us what we have been and what we are meant to be.

In an age made desperate by disjunction, these Holy Days call us to connectedness; to enter more deeply within our very selves; more fully into the lives of our people; more responsibly into the wider societies and the very planet that sustain us.

These holy seasons summon us both to responsibility and to freedom; to self-confidence as well as cooperation; to work and to play; to struggle and to peace.

These religious seasons come back to us each time the earth takes one more swing round its sun-star. And they never return without bringing in their wake three great questions for our lives. Whether we consider the Hebrew people in Egypt or Jesus at the climactic events of Jerusalem, we must invariably ask:

1. What brought them to this moment?
2. What sustains them in this moment?
3. What leads them beyond this moment?

And, as luck would have it, those are the self-same questions each of us needs to ask about our own lives at this privileged time of the year: queries about our own past, present, and future.

1. How did we get to be the persons we are today? What people, beliefs, situations, choices, evasions, commitments, or even failures went into the writing of our own personal scripts?

2. What resources, inner strengths and network of energies, structures and communities sustain us?

3. What power, vision, and imagination lead us along on our restless, pilgrim ways?

There may be as many answers to these questions as there are readers of these words. And yet the great traditions of our faith, the messages of Passover and Easter, speak consistently to us of redemptive capacities that we all share. They do not give us easy scripts for our days. But they insist that as we live out our lives, the great God of Life, subtle but unrelenting, stands by us, within us, around us. As God stood by the children of Israel; stood by Jesus.

We only glimpse this Genesis Force, this Passover God, this Easter Lord, through a glass darkly and from time to time. But it was enough for Moses and for Jesus. Maybe, just maybe, it can be sufficient for us as well.

They trusted profoundly while we, in Matthew Arnold's phrase, are "half believers of our casual creeds." They found grounds for hope, even in the midst of seeming darkness and absurdity. They imagined the better and strove to make it possible; we look at the chaos around us, throw up our hands and go into orgies of cynicism. They loved themselves and the people around them and beyond them with persistence; they cared for others personally and practically, not just abstractly; we so often tunnel into our own concerns, and grow hard of heart.

The great figures of our faith were restless until their pulses beat in tune with the very pulse of God. This God, both motherly and fatherly, is more patient than we; is almost certainly more gentle with us than we are with ourselves; most decidedly is not in the great hurry in which we usually find ourselves.

In short, all the intense, loving people God has caused to erupt in our midst—those that are famous and sung, and those countless unsung others treasured in only a few hearts now living—all of them lived out a quickened life undergirded by faith, by hope, by love.

For Christians, no matter how casual we may be, this Easter Day we celebrate calls us to probe within ourselves once again those three primal questions; to listen with care and patience to the One who is, for us, the fullness, the very revelation of who God is, and of what humanity might be. That Christ who trusted, hoped, and loved so persistently, has been propelled by God through death itself into the very *pleroma* or fullness of life. From that fullness of life that he achieved only by passing through the darkest valley, he now walks with us and calls to us to enter with him into the great struggle and the even greater mystery—

> with tough minds and tender hearts;
> with energy and equanimity;
> with courage and wit.

We are not here on this great day to celebrate abstractions or interesting moments from our common past. This is the Passover of each of our lives.

This is an Easter for us all.

This is the time, in the immortal words of both Horace (in Roman times) and Robin Williams (in *Dead Poets Society*), to seize the day . . . *Carpe Diem.*

To craft from this day a life.

And to discover in this life, the gracious glimpse of eternity.

YONDER

An Easter Reflection

In medieval Europe, historians report, it was possible to encounter a delightful, though rare, liturgical phenomenon: the *Risus Paschalis*—The Laughter of Easter. On Easter morning, the priest would rise in the pulpit and begin to tell the people jokes and stories until he had them in uncontrolled laughter. In our own time, Easter has been described as God's Cosmic Laugh or the feast of laughter from the tomb. For those who have fixated only on the solemnity of the paschaltide, the reminder of its levity comes as a happy and healthy counterpoint.

For most of us, our cultural memories of Easter might be of snappy clothes, brightly colored eggs, stuffed rabbits, and chocolate covered bunnies. These all suggest a world of kindness, security, renewal, and possibility. In a pressured and frantic time like our own, these are not unwelcome qualities.

But then we grew up one day, before we realized it. The clothes got grimy, worn, and outdated. The eggs had long since gone bad; the Hershey bunnies melted. If reality didn't kick us around the block a few times, at least we found ourselves disillusioned, depressed, sceptical about people and life.

Maybe we got a little sophisticated along the way and learned why we were treated to eggs and bunnies in the first place. Eggs, of course, are an ancient symbol of the renewal of life. The bunny, or at least the hare, was the creature born with his eyes open, and according to ancient legend, he was unblinking, too. He was seen as a night creature related to the moon. (Like the moon, the hare has a gestation period of 28 days.) Thus, the bunny was the creature who stood in the night and watched unblinking for the light to come. A lovely set of symbols, our hardened adult self might conclude, but are they anything more than that? Aren't they just more evidences of humanity's whistling in the cosmic dark? Well, they might be. Unless.

Unless somewhere along the way, in our growing up, we made some fundamental choice: to stand *in* life and *with* life and *for* life, no matter what it manages to throw in our path. No matter what thorns. No matter what crucifixions. We came to such a resolution precisely because we had intuited a fundamental fact: our life does not belong to itself alone. Paul wrote starkly in 1 Corinthians 6:19: "You do not belong to yourself." It is grounded in and graced by some Mystery that pulses in our blood, our fibers, our most profound longings.

We have entered, every one of us, into a process of living that calls the bluff on death every day—by forging the links of life on every side. Precisely as who we are and where we are. We go on. It is as Leonard Bernstein and Stephen Schwartz wrote in their musical *Mass* in 1971:

> When my plans all crumble
> And everything I have is gone.
>
> When my spirit falters
> On decaying altars
> And my illusions fail.
>
> I go on, just then.
> I go on, again.
> I go on to say,
> I will celebrate another day.

The Easter summons to go on, to trust even in the midst of adversity, to plunge more deeply into the fabric of living, echoes profoundly the Jewish celebration of Passover. Both events invite their celebrants into a timeless moment that can illuminate and transfigure all of time. They call us into a primal story, shocking us with the realization that this story is none other than our own.

At the Passover seder, the youngest child present asks why this night is different from all other nights, only to learn that this is the night when the Hebrew people were led by their gracious God from bondage to freedom; from lesser life to fuller life.

In the Easter Vigil, Christians are reminded that this is the night in which heaven is wedded to earth. This is the night on which Jesus delivered the first cosmic punch against death, the ancient enemy.

In both the Jewish and Christian ceremonies, for each of the faiths its most solemn moment, dramatic events are unfolded and described; events that might send Cecil B. DeMille or Stephen Spielberg salivating to their studios. But for all the drama involved in both the Passover and Easter liturgical accounts, the most stunning and mysterious item is a single word, and the smallest one at that. The word is the pronoun "this." *This* is the night. Not 3,000 years ago. Not 2,000 years ago. *This* is the night. As Edward R. Murrow used to say: You are There.

You are called—we are each of us called—into this transforming vision of life. Each of us is called with our own uniqueness to enter into the cosmic and personal drama, which Merton called the Dance of Life. We are called not in abstraction, but by name. Not just sometime. Not just somewhere. But in *this* place, *this* time, *this* situation.

As we grow older, we often come back to the starting point, back to the essentials. Back to the bunnies and the eggs and the chocolate. The bunny isn't just a bunny, you know. But it is that too, and we can enjoy it for what it is. And street people aren't just street people, you know. And plain old ordinary people aren't just ordinary, you know. And death isn't just death, you know. And the world isn't just the world, you know. And you, well you aren't just you.

This is one of the great shouting, boisterous, laughter-sustaining realities of these great feasts of Passover and Easter. Things aren't just what they seem to be. Whenever we labor to make things more than they are, more truthful, more beautiful, better, kinder, we have already signed on as a people of the more who will not settle for the less.

Risus Paschalis. The laughter of Easter. We have more right to that laughter, by God's gift, than all of the misery and mourning life can throw in our path. We grow up only to learn that the children were right after all, and better news still, we can always reclaim the child, crying and laughing in the deepest center of the self. We must become like little children, after all, to enter the Easter Kingdom.

On this day of all days, we must cast off our terrible solemnities, our constant frettings, our direst suspicions and scepticisms, and enter more deeply into the dance of our people and our God. In the undying dawn of Easter light, what right have we to cling to our dirges and diminishments?

In "The Golden Echo," nineteenth century Jesuit poet Gerard Manley Hopkins wrote:

> Weary, then, why should we tread?
> So care-coiled, so cumbered.
> When the thing we freely forfeit
>   is kept with fonder a care.
> A care kept—Where kept?
> Yonder, yes yonder.

Passover and Easter. Both are unrelenting in the lesson they never tire of teaching. That which is beyond is also and already here.

> Here to free us.
> Strengthen us.
> Motivate us.
> Caress us.
> Free us.

What do we have to laugh about at Easter? We of the twisted, befuddled, last years of the twentieth century? These words might sum it up:

> Yonder isn't just yonder,
>   you know.

A DIFFERENT DRUMMER
The Call of Pentecost

One of America's most revered and original thinkers, Lewis Mumford, died in the winter of 1990. He left behind him an autobiographical sketch in which he recalled the electric moment in his youth when he stood upon Brooklyn Bridge, literally to be transformed by what he saw and felt about him:

> Here was my city, immense, overpowering, flooded with energy and light; there below lay the river and the harbor, catching the last flakes of gold on their harbor. . . . And there was I . . . drinking in the city and the sky, both vast, yet contained in me, challenging me, beckoning me, demanding of me something that it would more take than a lifetime to give, but raising all my energies by its own vivid promise to a higher pitch. In that sudden revelation . . . I trod . . . with a new confidence that came not from my isolated self alone, but from the collected energies I had confronted and risen to.

In this moment that can only be called an epiphany, Mumford attained momentarily something of that experience for which all sensitive beings long: the instant when the dull waters of our lives seem transubstantiated into the headiest of wines; the flashing insight that brings illumination and power to a lifetime that might otherwise be reduced to a twilight existence at best; the mandate to achieve and fashion in life worthy things that matter and endure.

Surely it would not be wide of the mark to suppose that the first Pentecost was not only similar, but considerably more intense for those men and women who gathered together to await the

Spirit's charge. Thus, in fact, did Christianity begin: not with creeds and dogmas, even written gospels and popes. These would all quickly and helpfully flow from this spirited, initiating event that concentrated together the saving work of God in Christ. But first these earliest disciples had to reckon with the mighty emotional force unleashed in their own lives, and with their intense need to communicate its transforming power to others.

In particular, the personal and cosmic truths of the Resurrection of Jesus had come crashing into their own lackluster lives:

> that life is more than it seems on its often troubled surface;
>
> that death does not hold the trump card over our days and destinies—life does;
>
> that the story of Jesus is not his alone, but ours as well; his struggle, our struggle; his victory, our victory;
>
> that darkness, betrayal, desperation, even death itself could not hold Jesus down; and now these treacherous enemies could not hold them down either.

This faithful remnant could never again go back simply to business as usual. They had felt too deeply the quickening meaning and zest of their new lives. The forces of death and futility had been stared down in their very own hearts. Now even their business, relationships, and daily needs took on a new hue, coloration, and palpability.

All of this might be a funny or illogical way for a God to act, we might muse. But the New Testament doesn't call the Lord by the name of Logic. Rather, it designates our God with the name of Love. Some may find such a designation merely pious or sentimental. But for those who know something of the power and mystery of genuine love, the realization that God is precisely *that,* almost by definition, makes for a startling realization.

Love is mysterious. Personal. Intense. Definitional. We can never quite know, once it finds us, how it is going to leave us. Love can caress; it can also sting. Whatever else it may do, it will not leave us alone. That, precisely, is its power. It drives us to reach beyond our limits and selfish enclosures.

Whenever we take account of our loves and deep friendships over a long period of time, we often can discern a certain pattern to it all. In the beginning, there is frequent emotional expression of affection; but then things settle in for the long haul of faithfulness amid a welter of complexities and ordinariness. Doubts, questions, quarrels, and strains may develop. But love—if it is the genuine article—holds fast and true. It always seeks out again the fresh, the unwearied, and the possible.

Long-term loving is in itself an unending praise of all that persists in living. There may be dramatic moments along the way, but generally the course of love and friendship travels along unspectacular paths of constancy, encouragement, and mutual care. Some may find such a depiction of long-term love unspectacular and pedestrian. But without it, I suspect we would be profoundly different—and lesser—creatures.

Such an analysis might well be applied to yet another mystery, that of the Christian Church itself. It, too, begins with the emotional enthusiasm of Pentecost, the dramatic conversion of Paul, and many miracles and palpable signs of God's overwhelming nearness. But soon it settles in for the long haul of constancy, with its epiphanies coming less frequently.

The Church may not always offer the dazzling clarity and certainty of the noonday sun at all times, but it offers us a sustaining and ultimately saving panoply of sacrament, Scripture, structure, saints, sensibility, and so much else besides. With these, and the Church's constant invitation to mystical union with God, we have something akin to lightning flashes that illuminate the circling dimness of things, allowing us to see the terrain, and wander on our pilgrim way.

We ourselves are that mystery of the Church. A people who, in the middle of our little loves, small horizons, petty obsessions, and occasional downright meanness, get glimpses of the greater life terrain. At such moments, we are snapped out of our ordinariness by the mighty rush of the Spirit of God, and urged to achieve greater tasks. We are asked to dream dreams, casting from our lives mindlessness, mediocrity, and injustice. It is a blasphemy against God, wrote Jewish theologian Abraham Heschel, to say that God wants us to leave things just as we found them.

Living in this sometimes crazy world of ours with competence and kindness; with integrity and honesty; laboring where we can for new levels of justice and the survival of at least chastened ideals—

if Christians took such a mandate for achievement into their lives, they might leave a puzzled world wondering and inquiring: what makes them tick? Or to employ Thoreau's famous dictum that some people follow the beat of a different drummer, Christians may find the world around them pondering just what drummer beats the tune for their pulse of confidence, compassion, and service?

This, at last, is Christianity's trump card. Its believers hear and follow the divine Drummer, even if they do so faintly. We dance to that Drummer's tune, and invite others into its revelries and rhythms. Our invitation must always be extended with tolerance and breadth of vision. For in being the primal teacher, the Church must always be simultaneously the supreme learner and listener as well. Whenever believers become fanatical, self-righteous, and humorless, they stand at risk of losing not only their potential hearers, but their own God-given critical and questioning faculties as well.

Whenever we do admit the true, gentle power of the Spirit into our lives, we are liberated from self-insistence, the futile attempts to force meaning and happiness on our terms alone on our lives. We can become the mystery inside ourselves we are meant to be. We can become simpler, gentler, stronger, lighter, more just, more wise.

Such mystery waits within us, planted by God's own hand:

> yearning to breathe free;
>
> anxious to deliver us in a second birth;
>
> eager to transport us to a land of play and achievement, probing and peace.

Whenever we experience our own personal Pentecost, stand metaphysically upon our own version of the Brooklyn Bridge, we shall find ourselves coming to life again. And we will be able to listen anew to the intricate rhythms of that Divine Drummer who transfigures our nights and days.

THE BRINGING OF GOD TO BIRTH

Meditations on the Feast of the Assumption

Holy Mary, *Mother of God*. This is a phrase "cradle Catholics" learned to recognize about the same time they first dazzled their parents with the recitation of their ABC's. The words appear in all four major Eucharistic canons, and they reside in the center-piece of the Hail Mary as well. An expression used so repeatedly and persistently is not only a venerable one. Because of their very familiarity, such words are often likely to go unheard and unheeded as well.

Mother of God. That is an extraordinary phrase when you pause to puzzle over it. With its doctrinal intricacy and emotional power, it undoubtedly bears inside itself a range of meanings. But can such a seemingly arcane title speak convincingly to us, weary sojourners at the end of a troubled century?

The wording was hammered out in the fifth century and given final form at the Council of Ephesus in 431 in a famous theologi-cal phrase *theotokos*—bearer or mother of God. The bishops at Ephe-sus were determined to cling to this more radical phrasing rather than something milder, such as Mother of Jesus. At least two major issues were at stake:

Whether Jesus in himself was in truth the meeting of humanity and divinity?

Whether any human creature—Mary—could be given a title suggesting such unspeakable dignity?

Ephesus insisted on the affirmative in each case. That council, meeting over 1,500 years ago, spoke in many ways in a language different from our own. But on the basis of that assembly's intensity, and the persistence of the Marian instinct in the history of Catholicism, I would hazard a prediction.

In the second generation of post-conciliar Catholicism, we are going to witness a kind of renaissance of attention given to this amazing woman, called by Newman simply St. Mary. Protestants have been studying Mary anew in this ecumenical age, and many post-conciliar Catholics are likely to do the same. They may first have to distance themselves from some of the excesses of sentimentality in art and hymns to which they may have been exposed over the years. And just as young adults in our culture often develop a fresh appreciation of their parents when they have passed their own adolescent throes, seeing them in a newer, fuller perspective, so it well may be with cradle Catholics in their approach to Mary, the primal Mother.

There is a wealth of ways in which one might consider the insistent reach of Mary in the Catholic Christian heart:

1. As a remarkably strong, compassionate, and insightful woman in her own times.

2. As literally a saint, Queen of Saints, as the litany has it, and thus a transformed being who lives already a fuller life with God; one who is, accordingly, our contemporary, friend, and kindly intercessor.

3. As a spiritual and theological signifier or finger pointing to the figure of Christ . . . as graphically and tenderly commemorated in the icon tradition of the East.

4. As an inexhaustible image—or rather complexity of images—in the painting, sculptural, literary, musical, and devotional life in the history of Catholicism. The most powerful of these in our own age, most likely, is that rooted in the

Second Vatican Council's invocation of Mary as Mother or Model of the Church and humanity.

What is the portrayal of Mary, Mother of Jesus within the New Testament? It becomes immediately evident that she was a woman who knew a great deal about living: its pains, desperations, and contradictions. Having herself been a homeless one, even an exile, she lived under the expectation provided by Simeon that her own heart would be repeatedly pierced. And yet, Mary lived with the calm assurance that life was immeasurably more than its often murky present. In this life is to be found not only seeming tragedy, but triumph as well, and not just at some distant remove, but in the very heart of the hurly-burly.

Mary was equally at home at a party at Cana or under the Cross on Calvary. She proved herself to be, in the exchange with Gabriel, a careful questioner of events and annunciations: "How can this be . . . ?" And yet this Jewish maiden of Nazareth remained resilient, open, and trusting before the mystery of God's call and promise.

This one whom Gabriel designated "full of grace" brought up Jesus with profound attention to Jewish faith and life. She gave him not only physical birth but religious nurture. She loved him even when she couldn't fully understand. Luke puts on her lips the Magnificat, a paraphrase of Hannah's song in 1 Samuel 2. Taken together, the words of these women constitute one of the most scathing statements of social justice to be found anywhere in the Hebrew or Christian scriptures.

Dominican theologian Edward Schillebeeckx published in 1983 an essay titled "Magnificat: A Toast to God" in which he sees Mary's great utterance as a kind of primal prayer in the Jewish and Christian traditions: an openness to the visitation of God, that must be kept treasured life-long in our hearts . . . a prayer that mingles together praise, remembrance, and promise.

Mary's trust, of course, was to be repeatedly tested, most decidedly at the time of the crucifixion. When the situation was getting volatile, and the macho disciples fled in fear and panic, Mary was—to put it most simply—*there*. There as a supporting presence who trusted and endured.

Throughout the centuries, Christianity, or at least many major parts of it, have invested Mary with awesome titles. The litany in her honor describes her with adjectives and substantives in which most of us wish we could share at least a little: prudent, merciful, faithful, refuge, comforter, mirror of justice, cause of our joy.

The moving Salve Regina that still brings to a close the Church's evening Compline prayer of the Divine Office terms Mary "most gracious advocate" and "clement," presenting her to the faithful for what she is: literally a marvel to us in her own right and a consistent pointer to her son, Jesus.

In all, Mary is addressed by some forty-nine titles in the litany in her honor which has roots tracing back to the twelfth century. Its first printed edition most likely was that of Peter Canisius in 1558. That litany has a wonderful rhythmic and spiritual power to it. For those who grew up with its cadences, it can invite still a keen sense of the mysterious; can yet evoke a mystical world that is within us, around us, and beyond us with its imagery:

> Mystical Rose
> Tower of David
> Tower of Ivory
> House of Gold
> Ark of the Covenant
> Gate of Heaven
> Morning Star.

The litany invokes Mary as mother twelve times; virgin seven times; queen twelve times; and four times with architectural images portraying her as powerful and akin to persistent structures capable of lasting through time and, presumably, through the chaos that accompanies time.

Anyone who has triggered such an outpouring of devotion and poetical imagination over so many centuries must certainly have a strong emotional and spiritual appeal in our own time as well, if we would but scrutinize ourselves as well as our traditions. If the Church has long insisted that Mary is a special model of what it means to be human, then we need to take it seriously. The results could be explosive.

> *If* this strong and gentle woman whom so many centuries have addressed as Our Lady is truly the Mother of God.

> *If* we each in our own way are to be like her.

Then each of us is called to bring God to birth. In ourselves. In the world.

In a blending of grace or gift and personal action, we bring forth from ourselves the very seeds of God deep within us.

The re-conception of Christ in ourselves and our time is a venerable one in Christian thought and experience. It received a classic articulation in Gerard Manley Hopkins' verses in the late nineteenth century:

> Of her flesh he took flesh:
> He does take fresh and fresh,
> Though much the mystery how,
> Not flesh but spirit now
> And makes, O marvellous!
> New Nazareths in us,
> Where we shall yet conceive
> Him, morning, noon and eve;
> New Bethlems, and be born
> There, evening, noon and morn. . . .

Where is a more faithful, frightful, demanding Christian mandate to be found than here? Our task is joined to that of a God who shows to us both fatherly and motherly care, and who is laboring to come to birth:

> in the slums of hearts and the slums of cities;
> in corporations and in classrooms;
> in families and in friendships;
> in politics and budget castings . . .
> wherever humanity lifts its voice, takes its stand . . .
>   and longs to break forth from its shadows,
>   its scandals and its diminutions.

And what would it be but a blessed mother who nurtures in each of us the longing and resolve to stand as midwife—to help to bring to birth—a people and a world groaning in its pangs of insufficiency, exile, and expectation? Near the end of the Salve Regina, the faithful pray:

> And after this, our exile, show unto us the fruit of thy womb, Jesus. . . .

Pray for us, O holy Mother of God, that we may be made worthy of the promises of Christ.

Those ancient words constitute more than a prayer. They are for each of us a summons to transcend the draining limitations of our lives. They are an invitation that in our work and play, our coming and going, our living and dying, we may all be more worthy of the promises of Christ. Not least among those promises is that of the nativity of a new heaven and a new earth.

BLACK PACKARDS REELING

The Feasts of All Saints and All Souls

Every autumn, in the Catholic tradition, we observe two magnificent Days of Remembrance: All Saints and All Souls. They tend to snap us out of our usual humdrum in which we race around, constantly busy. These feasts focus our memories, our attention, and our direction, reminding us what our days are really for; insisting gently that we too must go where all those who have ever dwelt on the planet earth have preceded us. They have but gone down the road before us. If we had our own way, most of us would race through life pretending that no such road awaits us, beckoning to us to be one day its travelers.

The grievous times of individual death among family or friends punctuate the rest of the year for most of us as intensely personal versions of these Days of Remembrance. They tell us, with an unmistakable force, that there is a shadow always in attendance upon ourselves and those we love. Call it mortality. At one point and one point only does that shadow move ahead of the substance it attends. And we call that death.

These days of remembrance, though, would certainly be shallow ones if they did no more than teach us the obvious; if they only reminded us of that which we labor to forget. Rather, they have a livelier song to sing. Mortality always runs alongside us, it is true; but so does something else, something more. Call that something *destiny*, a gift and personal call from the God of Life.

Every time we sign ourselves with the Sign of the Cross, that sacred mark proclaims yet again that ours is a destiny that out-distances even death itself. That sacramental gesture is, for those of us who believe, our primal nonverbal annunciation of who we are, and who we are meant to be. For the Cross reminds us that our destinies involve the intersection and mingling of horizontal and vertical. The horizontal bespeaks our temporal lives in which we strive to do ordinary things well; the vertical indicates aspiration, a reaching for that realm where hope, promise, expectation, and spirit are saluted as facts of our experience every bit as profound as the cold shadow of mortality.

To those who know no better, it looks as if death is a one-time caller at each human heart and home. And if our entry into this world involves a trauma which we have forgotten, our departure from it leaves for those who have loved us a vacuum and a void that will ever be all too easily remembered.

Death comes not just once to us with its drama and cataclysmic separations. It shrieks out our name but once. But every day, it whispers to us, winks and beckons us look its way. The big black Packard of death pulls up at our door but once. But every day it circles our block or wanders through the suburbs of our lives.

Life and death sit silent partners each morning at our breakfast table, extending their cross-purposed invitations amid the newspaper sections, coffee, and bran muffins. They have their aliases, of course. Death dresses up in many disguises: as the temptation to mediocrity or narrowness; as the enlargement of self by the attempt to diminish others; as the urge to lodge our restless and immense passions in small and unworthy loves; as the willingness to drift through our days, not taking the energy or risk to plumb new friendships, purposes, or excitements.

Life, even on its shadow side, is more lyrical than death; for death, at the bottom line, is mute. At some times, life's music may sound a sad *adagio* in our hearts; at others, a lively *con brio* or *vivace*. But it always rides under us, this music of life, with its energies and counterpoints. "So we do not lose heart," the lyricist Apostle Paul wrote to his sometimes rowdy friends at Corinth, "our inner nature is being renewed every day" (2 Cor 4:16) NAV. "Life swallows up death.'' Even if there be days when as individuals we may be singing out of tune or even can no longer hear the orchestra, the life-music will not be stilled; it refuses ultimately to go unsung.

This is the faith that braced and comforted our own mothers and fathers when they came face-to-ugly-face with sorrows and losses so scalding that no words alone could ever probe the inner devastation they left behind. This faith in the Christic song of life that will never go unsung has sustained one hundred generations of believers in the tradition that we know as Christianity. Its melody is, in fact, a finer variation on an ancient anthem long chanted by the human family in its long sojourn on the earth.

This faith, too, finds an echo in lines Theodore Roethke wrote in 1964:

> I walk between dark and dark
> My soul nearly my own.
> My dead selves singing
> And I embrace this calm. . .
> I am most immoderately married
> The Lord God has taken my heaviness away.

When we allow even our deadest self to sing the song of the Christ, we too may find something of our heaviness lifted. For we shall have entered that realm in which inner burdens are lifted, courage can run free, and black Packards are sent reeling back into the dark from which they came.

Section Two
MORE HUMAN LIVES

TO SEARCH FOR AUTHENTICITY

American Securities— False and True

Consider the words of a shrewd observer of the American scene. If you're an unrepentant optimist, you may want to get a grip on the arms of your chair:

> As a people, we are wanting in respect . . . we lack reverence. We are too ready to persuade ourselves that all is well so long as wealth . . . increases. We seek facile solutions to the great problems. There is not now and never has been a civilized people. Ignorance, sin, depravity, deceit, greed, and selfishness have always prevailed and still prevail in the world. The majority has never loved nor does it now love trust and mercy . . . and holiness.

This is Bishop John Lancaster Spalding orating in 1902 in an address called "A National Calamity" given after the assassination of President McKinley. Kentucky-born Lank Spalding was in his time one of American Catholicism's most articulate, intellectual—and believe it or not—liberal voices.

Spalding sounds remarkably like one of the chorus of critics of American life in our own era . . . whether it be a novelist like Tom Wolfe in *Bonfire of the Vanities*, a skilled film-maker like Woody Allen in *Crimes and Misdemeanors*, or a whole stable-full of essayists, including Paul Kennedy, Robert Nisbet, Max Lerner, Barbara Tuchman, or Joseph Campbell. He even sounds a lot like Thomas Merton who could be as much acid critic as gentle spiritual director. In a 1966 article titled "Is the World a Problem?" Merton described the human condition in the following terms:

> . . . turbulent, mysterious, demanding, exciting, frustrating, and confused. . . . [This is a world in which] almost nothing is really predictable, in which most definitions . . . become incredible even before they are uttered, in which people suffer together and are sometimes utterly beautiful, at other times, impossibly pathetic. . . . [A world in which] there is much that is frightening, in which almost everything public is patently phony, and in which there is at the same time an immense ground of authenticity.

That last stroke—an immense ground of authenticity—is the touch of the incurable Christian humanist. The same note of hope is found in Spalding, too, as he rounds out his picture of America in the quote with which we began:

> We more than any other people are dedicated to the securing of the largest freedom, the completest justice to all, to men and women, to the strong and the weak, to the rich and the poor.

The Christian humanist is always drawn both to stark realism and to enduring hope. All well-informed believers of good will can survey the American scene and find a nation with highly articulated ideals. We were, after all—in the full flush of the Enlightenment—the first country to define itself into existence. The same observers can look out on a vast historical reservoir of goodness and justice that Americans have manifested in their personal and corporate lives.

But they know all too well the catalogue of our frequent and ongoing failures. They know the stats. About crime, drugs, homelessness, AIDS deaths, hunger, abortions, promiscuities, infidelities, intensifying racism, sexism, environmental devastations. There is truly both a bright and a shadow side to this land that Lincoln was pleased to call, in 1862, "the last best hope of Earth." And it is to this troubled American land that the gospel—with all its sting, its challenge, and its comfort—needs to be spoken comprehensively and compellingly in our time.

The great religious traditions of this country have healing words to speak, saving acts to perform in the midst of America's disarray. For example, all three major faiths of the West, Judaism, Christianity, and Islam, hold in common the Decalogue or Ten Commandments as a primal moral code. The first commandment, forbidding false gods, takes full awareness of the human tendency to pursue the quite legitimate need for security in ways that are ultimately debilitating and devastating.

Not surprisingly, people of all times—and of our time in particular—try to substitute such false deities as success, comfort, excitement, pleasure, radical individuality, or self-sufficiency as supposed guarantors of happiness and security. Who are better poised in American life than thoughtful believers to suggest the futility of placing false ultimacies along these paths? And where are to be found better institutions than the religions—even with their own flaws and insufficiencies—to suggest attitudes and life-styles more faithful to the deepest human needs of individual and community alike?

The ancient faiths can build on the nation's strengths and challenge its weaknesses in countless ways. The Triple Crown of Christian virtues, faith, hope, and charity, would serve well as effective foils to many of the misplaced intensities of our time:

> Faith or fidelity can challenge our shallow approach to commitment, our easy assumptions that we have "one life to live" and must force contentment from it at whatever cost.

> Hope and renewed imagination can help to reduce our frantic drives to accomplish all things *now,* regardless of the stress or betrayals involved.

> Love and creativity can assault the gnawing fear that beneath all our technologies, sophistications, and frantic pace, nothing lurks but ultimate emptiness.

Should faith, hope, and love strike you as just too traditional, just too tame to invoke in the revivifying of a people, flip these virtues over. Imagine, if you can, an integrated person, or a just nation built on their opposites. Built on Futility instead of Faith; on Despair instead of Hope; on Indifference and Hate instead of Love. Faced with that living hell, we all might develop a deepened enthusiasm for the old Christian Triple Crown.

But none of these virtues will play in abstraction. They have to take living, breathing, full-blooded form, or they will never compel, never seduce, never achieve. We all know the unspoken word here; these realities need to be *incarnated;* need to take up residence in hearts and lives; in families and communities; in societies and nations.

Will such believers cast their lives and energies into such an enterprise? Or will they have to send their regrets, announcing that they were otherwise occupied? If they cannot rise to the challenge, Spalding's nation "dedicated to the securing of the largest freedom, the completest justice to all" may well find its people perplexed, its prospects diminished, and its promise ever unredeemed.

TO COMFORT AND
TO CHALLENGE
All Things Human

All things human, given enough time, go badly. . . .

This seemingly dismal phrase is attributed to one of the most respected and ecumenically progressive of twentieth century American Catholic thinkers. An odd thought, one may think, for a progressive. It sounds a shatteringly discordant note in the supposed symphony of modern progress. It makes a reactionary noise that might lead us to turn away in a kind of righteous horror.

And yet, these words grab onto us much like Coleridge's Ancient Mariner whose craggy hand just refuses to let go. In most of our own range of experiences, there is just enough of the ring of truth here to give us pause. We have all felt Melville's "deep drizzly November" in the soul. Our plans, expectations, projects, hopes, and careers—don't they have a way of going awry, even of coming unstuck?

Even the happiest and longest of life's game-plans seem to reach their final innings in such places as trauma units, oncology wards, or CCU's. We find ourselves in well-upholstered suburban funeral homes, muttering lines about a friend tragically lost, who looks natural . . . or who is now beyond the pale of suffering. We feel trapped in the darkest of deep wells, with no foothold secure enough to rise. We shake our heads, hug the relatives, and feel relieved when we can take to our cars, strike out on the express-way, far away for a time from the house of death.

We all find it difficult at times to accept those diminishments and contradictions that were not included in our youthful game-plans. Even though with the experience of maturity we come to distinguish those factors in living that can be challenged and changed, and those that cannot, we still may feel angry and bludg-eoned by events and circumstances. It takes a special wisdom to realize that we are given the frames and canvases of our lives; our task lies in bringing, as far as we are able, color and vibrancy to the picture. The definition of who we are is linked intimately not so much to our situations in life, as to our creative responses to them.

In particular, we often find it most problematical to accept our own inner weaknesses. We are especially unforgiving to ourselves, and thus deprive ourselves of those inner acceptances that could enable us either to labor for the better or to endure with patience, courage, and hope. Few thinkers of our time have better articulated this need for a transforming self-acceptance than psychologist Carl Jung. In *Civilization in Transition,* he wrote:

> Recognition of the shadow . . . leads to the modesty we need in order to acknowledge imperfection. . . . Perhaps this sounds very simple, but simple things are always the most difficult. In actual life it requires the greatest art to be simple, and so acceptance of the self is the essence of the moral problem and the acid test of one's whole outlook on life.

> That I feed the beggar, that I forgive an insult, that I love my ene-my in the name of Christ, all these are undoubtedly great vir-tues. . . . But what if I discover that the poorest of all beggars, the most impudent of all offenders . . . that these are within me, and that I myself stand in need of the alms of my own kindness, that I myself am the enemy who must be loved. What then?

The realization of our plight and insufficiencies are hardly unique to our own times. Consider Jeremiah: that unquiet revolu-tionary who lived in the seventh and sixth centuries before Christ. "And so they took Jeremiah and threw him into the cistern . . . and Jeremiah sank into the mud" (Jer 38:6) NAV. Across twenty-seven centuries, we see our plight in that of the ancient prophet.

Jeremiah lived in Judah, the remnant of conquered Israel. The Assyrians had already battered away most of the rest of David's ancient kingdom. Judah now stood alone, not unlike Britain in 1940 with the dark forces of Nazidom closing in all around.

In Jeremiah's time, in that ancient cauldron of the Middle East, the blitz was about to begin. And Jeremiah called the shot with deadly accuracy. For his forthrightness in a grisly time, for his fearless speaking of the truth to power, Jeremiah found himself cast into a vasty deep with no means of escape. All around him, things were falling apart. The old structures—political and religious—were tottering wildly. Jeremiah had judged the powers of his own time guilty of grave evils. He looked about him and saw many of the religious securities of his own tradition crumbled: temple, priesthood, kingship, and centralized worship. Everywhere he looked, disaster loomed. And then came the pit and the mud. All things human, given enough time, go badly.

Jeremiah stared all this disaster in the teeth. But in seeing it all, he saw something more. It was precisely that vision that made him both prophet and theological revolutionary. He saw the crisp power of God's energy and human resourcefulness as being, in fact, absolutely unlimited. If the Law of God can be found no longer in the books, then it must be sought out as inscribed on the heart. Writes biblical scholar John L. McKenzie: "This wild conception of intimate union with God is scarcely paralleled elsewhere in the Old Testament." For those who may have forgotten the end of the biblical story, the king eventually orders Jeremiah yanked up out of his cylindrical prison.

No surprise then, that Jesus, drenched in Jewish tradition and Jeremiah's words, would at times speak words of challenge along with his comfort. As Luke reports, Jesus says "I have come for division" (Luke 12:51) NAV. He realized that his demanding message might at times divide families, friends, and nations. The gospel message, after all, insists that there come those moments at which we must take a stand. If you don't stand for something, Bruce Springsteen said in a memorable moment, you're going to fall for anything.

If the gospel message doesn't sometimes shake us, cast the very meaning of our lives before us, then it is at bottom no news at all—certainly not *good* news. The gospel has to speak more to us than cotton-candy pieties if it is to transform our shadow lives into depth and substance.

The gospel forces us to probe these lives of ours . . . to see our days, our communities, our world, in vaster perspective. If everything about our lives is merely business as usual . . . if our actions and attitudes are not shaped notably by our faith . . . then either the Word has not been well-spoken to us, or we have failed to listen to it seriously.

All good things, given enough time, go badly. The gospel confronts us with this undeniable fact: Bethlehem leads to Calvary. And Calvary to Easter. Our lives, like that of the Jesus we profess to follow, is an ongoing redemptive process—from cradle to cross to resurrection.

When things go badly, we come face-to-face with our own poverty. We confront the hollowness and charades that so often go into our living. We are invited to pass over from hollowness to hallowedness. And in this crossing over, we are driven to seek out new realities both within and without ourselves. We find ourselves in search of clarity, charity, compassion, and justice. We discover ourselves eager to drink of the unquenchable spring with which the God of Life graces our very being. It was the crystal water of this self-same source that sustained Jeremiah, even when he was sunk in his tank of slime.

For us, as for Jeremiah and Jesus, the pit or cross or tomb is but a comma in our lives, not a period. Jeremiah soared from his entrapment—scarred, but strong—to face a new day. At the bottom of the pit, faith finds not its conclusion, but its confirmation. In such crucibles of our lives, realistic hope takes root and flowers. There too, genuine charity—not just the sentimental variety—begins to transform our days.

> We are all in some way in the miry cistern.
> We are all on the cross.
> We are all eventually broken like bread.
> We all are crushed and poured out like wine.

All who gather for Christian Eucharist come together—however dimly they may perceive or articulate it—in search of solace and strength in the midst of life's darksome realities. We come hither with our weakness and nakedness, our hopes and resolves. We arrive suffering from a hunger that the small hors d'oeuvres of daily life can never satisfy.

In our brokenness, we are given a spur to wholeness.

In our loneliness, we are granted an intimation of what true amity might be.

In our irresolution and wavering, we are given sustenance, security, and hope.

And in our life's wandering, we are offered a vision of what our ultimate home might be: that realm where all things human go—not badly, but—toward the shaping of a new humanity, recast in the image and likeness of the Refining and Compassionate God.

TO TOUCH THE SCARS
The Surprises of the Obvious

Have you ever gone looking for your glasses and found them on top of your head? Searched for your car keys and spotted them finally in your back pocket? Forgot a good friend's last name just when you had to make an introduction? Embarrassing moments. Could be middle-age setting in. More likely, it's just part of our human condition peeping through. We often miss the obvious.

Rarely is that message so clearly announced in the New Testament as in the Emmaus story reported in the 24th chapter of Luke. Two unnamed disciples of Jesus are making their way along the road to Emmaus when they are joined by a stranger. He walks with them, talks with them, even offers them a sweeping review of their bible history. Only when they sit down to break bread with the stranger do they recognize that he is the Christ in their midst. And at that very moment, he vanishes from their sight.

The travelers in the gospel story missed the obvious, that their companion on the road was Jesus. But by story's end, they had learned something profound that would reshape their lives utterly. They had learned that the obvious is not the all: that those things we think to be most immediate to us are only part of life. That life has other dimensions within it, around it, beyond it.

This passage is fascinating for at least a couple of reasons. First, it's one of the few humorous moments in the New Testament. It shows Jesus as something of an actor and stand-up comedian.

There he is, the one who was at the center of the events of that terrible weekend. And he's the one who deadpans it: *O really, what went on in Jerusalem this weekend?* We remember that he knew his psalms; and the 2nd psalm refers to *a God who laughs.*

We realize, too, that he knows full well what happened; he needed for the meaning of those days to come alive in them, so that they could express it well for themselves and for others. This is yet another of those *Who Do You Say That I Am?* moments. A probing and confronting moment. The disciples have to interpret—and now each of us has to interpret—just what happened in those days in first-century Jerusalem that might change our lives in late twentieth-century America.

Second, this is about the only time in the New Testament that the seemingly tough, macho disciples drop their guard and let us see inside their feelings. It's no secret that they could be dim-witted. And when they finally figure out what's going on, they also realize that when they heard their guest speak, their hearts burned within them—a fire in the belly that they used to get when Jesus used to talk with them. Just when we thought they were like tough-guy Hollywood extras sent over from central casting, we find traces of Orson Welles and James Earl Jones stored up inside their Galilean hearts.

There are lessons for all of us in the Emmaus story. We can all be dim-witted in our own way. Can fail to see the obvious. Can be in such a rush to have more; get more; be always living for tomorrow; think that our life will begin only when all our ducks line up in a row; when we've made things go our way. We don't see the possibilities within us; the presences around us. Not only don't we see the Christ in our moments. We often don't see one another; listen to one another; enjoy one another; heal and help one another.

Such a blockage of the physical senses inevitably interrupts our spiritual sensibility as well. No one perceived or proclaimed this more clearly than the Jesus of the gospels. In one of the most dramatic post-resurrection scenes of the New Testament, Jesus passes into the locked room of his frightened followers, calls the doubting Thomas to his side and bids him touch his scars. If you would believe, Jesus seems to say, you need not have all life's puzzles solved, whether they be personal or cosmic. When Thomas doubts,

Jesus does not lecture or scold. Rather he does the simplest thing of all. He tells Thomas to come *touch* the marks of his style of life . . . to live out his brand of living. Then belief may well come in its turn. Questions and seeming doubts may well be the metals of which deeper faith is forged. Only through such an intimate— and at times terrifying—touching can one's life be truly "hidden with Christ in God" (Col 3:3).

When we do not dare to touch his scars, we shrink at the same moment from touching either others or ourselves. The gospel truth enshrines a stunning irony: when we bottle up our lives within ourselves, we lose them. Only when we start to give ourselves away do we at last come to any sort of self-possession. Only then do we discover who we truly are. And that new self is deeper and truer than the one we left behind.

These are some of the ordinary things that Jesus did so extraordinarily well: he saw and listened; sometimes wept and sometimes enjoyed with others; he healed and he helped. He went around doing good. Every time we break his bread, we touch again his scars. And he touches us in turn with his sensibility and splendor.

Here is surely to be found one of the basic meanings of Eucharist. By taking it into ourselves, we enter the Christic moment. It becomes our moment. This is the sacrament of Emmaus. The eternal in the instant. The extraordinary in the ordinary. God's kingdom breaking into our lives.

A popular song appeared with the musical *The Wiz* some years ago. It told us, with rhythmic insistence: You got to get on down . . . get on down the road. And so we must. The road to Emmaus. The road that takes us to tomorrow, but only through a today well and fully lived. It is mystical, yet realistic, this pathway that leads us to our only true liberation. It leads us to that land where we are startled, zen-like, into an awareness of the obvious. And where we are enlightened at last about its possibility and its power.

TO CAST OUT FEAR
Enter Lazarus Laughing

In 1927, playwright Eugene O'Neill was engrossed in the writing of a play freighted with religious concern. While some Americans watched their stock tickers, and others followed the solo Atlantic flight of Charles Lindbergh, O'Neill had become fascinated with the biblical figure of Lazarus, the man Jesus had brought back from the grave.

What would life be like for a man who had passed beyond the borderland of death? Would he be morose? Metaphysical? Self-righteous? Unrelentingly serious? None of the above, O'Neill decided. "There is only laughter," the astonished stage Lazarus reports. "Fear is no more." So it was that O'Neill called one of his least known works by an unlikely title: *Lazarus Laughed*.

Fear is no more. An extraordinary statement. The casting out of fear, in fact, is one of the most pervasive themes in both the Jewish and Christian scriptures. It is to be found in Isaiah (35:3-4):

> Strengthen all weary hands,
> steady all trembling knees
> and say to all faint hearts:
> Courage. Do not be afraid.
> Look. Your God is coming.

The exhortation to put aside fear runs through the New Testament from the Annunciation to the post-Resurrection appearances of Jesus. In between, in the Apostolic Discourse of the tenth chapter of Matthew, Jesus urges his listeners no less than three times not to be afraid. And in the twelfth chapter of Luke, he admonishes: "There is no need to be afraid, little flock, for it has pleased your Father to give you the Kingdom."

To enter into the life of faith, into the heart of the gospel, is to take that admonishment with all the seriousness and freedom that the individual can muster. To cast out fear and gird on courage is to make the primal plunge into the Christ-life.

Fear brings considerably more in its wake than only emotional distress; it can paralyze us at several levels of self-perception:

> Personally:
> that we are unworthy, and unlovable; that our inadequacies will always overtake our talents.
>
> Professionally:
> that we can never attain anything resembling excellence in the field to which we have been called.
>
> Socially:
> that the world is in a hopeless and unredeemable tangle; that our crises of injustice, hunger, economic imbalance and nuclear and ecological danger are insurmountable and not worth our best efforts.
>
> Cosmically:
> that the universe itself is but a theater of pointlessness, absurdity, and futility.

The cacophony of terrors that loudly screech or subtly insinuate themselves both within us and around us are killers. They can tear out the veins and slash the very arteries of the insistent pulse of life and holiness that is God's unrelenting call to all of us on this troubled planet. Over against such chaos, in stark opposition to these principalities and powers, rings the majestic, magisterial voice of the one Christianity calls Lord. It is Christ Jesus who tells his followers with devastating simplicity: "Fear is useless. What is needed is trust" (Mark 5:36) NAV.

The Christ comes forth in the scriptures and in Christian tradition and piety as the primal one who faces down fear, and who comes at living with a fullness of heart. In his person, he overcomes the death or downward pull that assaults us not only on the last day that we breathe, but throughout our experience while we live on earth. He is the one who truly *sees* beneath surfaces and appearances, and enables us to see as well.

It is hardly accidental that the great spiritualities of the world so often associate themselves with mountains and heights. (Our very word "altar" derives from the Latin *altus,* meaning high.) These are linked, of course, to the tradition of *axis mundi,* the sacred space of meeting of the divine with the human. But the sacredness of Sinai, of Tabor (the mount of Transfiguration), of Calvary itself speaks of something more. People of faith are also people of the mountain in the sense that they can see just a bit farther, just a bit more clearly into the heart of things.

Those who are eager to see so profoundly are also a people ready to venture forth on the three great steps of genuine spirituality. Classically, these are called the purgative, illuminative, and unitive ways. But they could also be described as three steps or imperatives of spiritual awareness:

1. Admit that reality is not just what it appears so often to be: aging, suffering, injustice, and death.

2. Search out an answer to the resultant question: what, then, *are* things? Christian faith answers that things are as the Christ sees and says them to be.

3. Enter into Christ's world of vision and values, making them our own, each in our own unique and unrepeatable way.

But to follow these paths, to climb these heights, we must first follow the Christ into the desert where fear is conquered. The same Jesus who opens the eyes of the blind, the ears of the deaf; who brings Lazarus back to his persistent, argumentative, and loving sisters, would have us open our own eyes and begin to lead transfigured lives:

that share rather than clutch;

that are compassionate rather than self-obsessive;

that long for justice and not just comfort;

that aim for excellence and not just mediocrity.

This is an agenda that both attracts and terrifies. It would, in fact, be nothing but the most cruel of illusions unless the energies of God both under-ride and out-ride us. We can pursue such a life-goal only if there be a loving divine heart who knows our hearts and cares clear through. As southern novelist Reynolds Price noted in a recent interview, there is only one question that really engages serious human attention: is there a God and does that God care for me? An earlier writer, D. H. Lawrence had come surprisingly close to the same thought in a poem called "Pax." All that truly matters, Lawrence wrote:

> . . . is to be at one with the living God.
> To be a creature in the house of the God of life.

To dwell in such a house is to be able to affirm with the poet Wordsworth that the human heart can be one thousand times love-lier than the world in which it dwells. It is to pass beyond the tyranny of the moment and live our lives with the endless equanimity of untroubled hearts. It is to break forth from our self-imposed tombs, and emerge into that light to which Jesus introduced Lazarus.

Then, like Lazarus, we might enjoy a cosmic laugh, and get on with our comic, serious business of living. Such a task will join us intimately with all those who are convinced that the kingdom of God lies truly within and around them, urging them onward to those heights where the imagination fails, and God is all in all.

TO MAKE THE SPIRIT VISIBLE
The Incarnational Imperative

He descended into Hell.
(The Apostles' Creed)

This stark and startling phrase from the Apostles' Creed traces its roots biblically to the First Epistle of Peter. Theologians have busied themselves with its implications for centuries, and biblical commentaries offer a smorgasbord of possible interpretations. Metaphorically, the imagery of this cosmic scene can still rivet the spiritual imagination, inviting reflections on the fathomless, incarnational reach of Christ into the human condition.

As I use the term "hell" in these ruminations, it refers not so much to that place or condition Dante described so graphically and unforgettably where those who enter must abandon all hope. Rather I refer to a more popular usage of the term in which it comes to mean a life that seems to border on death itself by its familiarity with isolation, turmoil, and pain. From such a point of view, the Christ can be said to have entered the precincts of hell not only dramatically after his death on the cross, but repeatedly throughout his public career.

He descended into hell. We have all resided in that infernal city or its suburbs at times in our lives. One of the truest securities of Christian faith is that whenever we enter within its suffocating confines, we do not go there alone. Christ is there with us. Not just in metaphor. Not just in soothing image. Not even in some

69

theological sleight of hand. He is there with us totally. Into the very teeth of that hell he has experienced so fearsomely, Jesus preaches about the power of a kingdom that can overcome it. That kingdom too he has known full well in his own heart and experience, and into it he bids us enter.

Put simply, he is with us. In our turmoils and in our revelries. He is in our colony of time—to use a striking image of Dr. Martin Luther King, Jr.—but as herald of that eternal empire in which he dwells. He is in that kingdom now, bearing in his person the one thing in heaven made by human hands: scars.

Just how fully the Christ's body bore the marks of human cruelty are all too obvious for those who have become familiar with the passion narratives of the gospels:

> The Hands of Jesus:
>> that opened the scrolls of the prophets
>> that reached out to lepers
>> that made the broken whole
>> that washed others' feet . . .
>
> Those same hands were punctured, pounded with spikes, and matted with blood.
>
> The Feet of Jesus:
>> that took him to the holy places of his faith
>> to dinners and wedding parties
>> to the remotest places where people were in need
>> into the company of the marginal, the outcast, and the
>>> forgotten
>> to places of natural beauty and refreshment
>> to courts of law and power where he refused to back away
>>> from his vision and purpose . . .
>
> Those feet were smashed, mangled, and drained of their life's blood.
>
> The Heart of Jesus:
>> that saw a new vision of human possibility
>> that wept over his friends and his people
>> that apparently was so witty and kindly that children
>>> flocked to be near him
>> that he gave in utter trust into the will of the Father . . .
>
> That heart was pierced with a lance.

He is with us. Not just we live, Paul tells us. Christ lives in us. His Spirit moves in our days and nights. In our scars. In our rejoicings. In our struggles to be better than we are. He reaches out that we might link our own hands with his. He motions us to walk in his footsteps. He offers an intimacy so close that our pulse might beat in rhythm with his heart, with the very heart of God. Thus are we summoned to be the incarnational presence of Christ in our place and time. For the flesh, wrote poet Theodore Roethke, "can make the spirit visible."

Christ offers us a power, a vision, and a possibility for ourselves that we likely could never conceive on our own. He urges us, as did Ezekiel of old, to leave our self-imposed graves to enter into the companionship and pursuits of the gracious. With them we may set about our own liberation by helping to liberate others from the numberless snares of death and limitation that beset individuals and societies on all sides.

Jesus offers such powers for liberation as the English Romantic poet Shelley invoked in his nineteenth-century verse:

> To suffer woes which Hope thinks infinite;
> To forgive wrongs darker than death or night;
> To defy Power which seems omnipotent;
> To love and bear; to hope 'til Hope creates
> From its own wreck the thing it contemplates;
> Neither to change, nor falter, nor repent;
> This like the glory, Titan, is to be
> Good, great and joyous, beautiful and free.
> This is alone Life, Joy, Empire and Victory.
>
> *(Prometheus Unbound,* Act IV)

The highly unorthodox Shelley might well have been depicting the empire and victory of Christ in this rendering of one who had suffered torments unspeakable, yet who held steadfastly to those kindly unseen realities that make the seen both possible and precious. Jesus knew that humanity has not only an inner life—the emotional and psychological—but that that very interiority itself has an inner life where the transcendent God lingers, dwells, urges, comforts, and calls. With that bedrock assurance and trust the Lord Jesus, having descended into hell itself, can stand with us now in whatever anguish may afflict our lives.

Haven't we all had a moment in life when the realization came upon us that someone we had taken for granted, had never appreciated sufficiently, had been there all along, quietly, unconditionally there *for us?* Such a moment of realization can be sobering, humbling, and exhilarating, all in one. What else do Christians mean when they call Jesus their Lord, Savior, Lover, Friend than that they have found him to be just such a steadying, transcendent presence?

All the images of Jesus from Good Shepherd to Sacred Heart have sought to evoke in faithful believers the same realization that such a tough and tender lover shares their lives. That same Jesus has joined his infinitude to our immediacies, and cares for each of us, moment by moment. He is the intense manifestation of that very God whom John Henry Newman once described as being everywhere as absolutely and entirely as if He were nowhere else.

"Whether we be young or old," Wordsworth wrote in the *Prelude:*

> Our destiny, our being's heart and home
> Is with infinitude, and only there;
> With hope it is, hope that can never die,
> Effort and expectation and desire
> And something evermore to be.

For the faithful heart, that something evermore is not an abstraction, but the reality of the living Christ, the image of the Invisible God. He who walked the road to Calvary before us, and ratified God's final victory over futility and death. That same Jesus not only descended into hell. But as medieval writers loved to observe, he brought about the harrowing of hell; that is to say, he plundered it of its lock on human destinies.

With the grace of that Jesus stirred within us, we too could labor for liberation from those private hells in which all of us dwell at some times. We, too, could pass over from death to transfigured life. That is the meaning, ultimately, of *salus:* salvation, health, healing, grace, and wholeness. It is mightier far, St. Paul assures us, than all the forces of sin and suffering. *Salus* prods and pursues us. Bursts our limits. Harrows our hells. Bids us follow the incarnational imperative: to become the body and blood of Christ in our time and place. Do we listen? Do we dare?

TO BE TRANSFORMED
The Bridges of Our Lives

As you drive north out of my hometown of Louisville across the interstate Kennedy Bridge, you are surrounded with bridges both to the left and right, all crossing the mighty Ohio River. Beneath you flows one of America's major waterways, winding its steady way to the Mississippi and then to the sea. Visible below on the Kentucky shore lurks the cobblestone wharf where slaves labored, and where Jackson, Lincoln, Emerson, Whitman, and Melville trod; where soldiers of both the Union and the Confederacy embarked on steamboats carrying them off to battle in the Civil War.

Ahead lies southern Indiana, still technically Canada by terms of the Quebec Act, at the time the city was founded in 1778. Off to the left, just barely in sight, lie the ancient rock formations of the Falls with coral reefs and fossil beds dating back, geologists say, some three hundred million years.

When the bridge traffic slows to a rush hour crawl, I find that it mutes frustration and cools the temper to give vent to a few ruminations, even cosmic thoughts. The site, after all, has enough ancient associations to keep the imagination busy.

In particular, those three bridges, converging nearly to a point on the northern shore, give me pause. They bring to mind the three critical bridges or connections that converge to give balance and significance to a life. All of us share a profound need to belong to forces greater than ourselves alone. The primal hungers to break

73

forth from our loneliness, to find true intimacy in life, find expression in a trio of relationships:

> We need to belong to our own hidden better selves
> —despite our own frequent self-betrayals.
>
> We need to belong compassionately to one another
> —despite our posturings of radical individualism.
>
> We need to belong ultimately to God
> —despite the busy sophistication of our seeming self-sufficiencies.

All these radical needs of the human heart, if we attend carefully to them, cast us on the ground of mystery—precisely the precincts where many of us would choose not to enter. For a time, we can usually insulate ourselves from mystery's call with our careers, professions, or general busyness. And yet, a sudden crisis, a religious experience, a mid-life transition—any of these can pierce our armor, bringing us face-to-face with the ultimate questions and relationships of a life.

Once we arrive on the mystical shore, though, if we are fortified with the traditions of faith, we discover that mystery may indeed be not our enemy, but our ally. We begin to appreciate more fully that one of the greatest treasures of Christian faith is that it takes us beyond the murkiness and vagaries so often associated with the realms of the mysterious. Those of us who are believers find that while mystery is not fully unveiled, neither is it a stranger, for it has a Christic face and heart. In this world we may be but afloat on an insecure raft, but the current of the great good river carries us forward, and we can trust ourselves to its divinely driven currents.

Particularly as we pass what are generally considered the middle years of a life, we find that we re-orient both our values and perspectives. If the first half of a life is often passed with the underlying assumption that we must make so much of the earth belong to and answer to ourselves; then the second half often brings with it the insight that we belong to the earth and the God who set it in motion. In the second half of our lives, we seem to see as with new eyes:

> What we have lost in energy
> —we may have gained in perspective.

What we have lost in our own plans and expectations
—we may have found redefined, fashioned more in the divine plan than our own.

What we have lost in self-centered scheming
—we may have recovered in trust, freedom, and hope.

The time of life after the so-called "mid-life crisis" may well be that in which we rediscover the lure of sacraments as those saving acts that offer us a more intimate entrance into the obvious. We discover that those things we thought to be obvious were really nothing of the sort. Not only is the obvious not the all; it is not even anymore obvious. As we gather some age about ourselves, we begin to grasp with just a bit more insight and grace the nature of the inner cargo we have borne unaware in our earlier life. We discover that our personal stories are laden with intricacies and meanings deeper than we ourselves could either narrate or comprehend. We begin to sense that death—which on the mere surface of things seems to stalk and rule and ruin—can itself be conquered. Its vanquishment comes only when the grim reaper is embraced as it was by the Christ, himself a victim of mortality in his "middle" years.

As we ponder anew in our own middle years the great questions of life, we wonder if scattered pieces we have found of the cosmic puzzle fit somehow together. Our faith has ready an answer as simple as it is profound. What's it all about? What's it all for? Everything exists for God. Is that too pious, too facile a response? Perhaps.

Ask more, then. What is God for? According to God, at least as recorded in the Old and New Testaments, God stands for us, in the intimacy of a marriage covenant. Thus, by a kind of mystical syllogism it follows that everything exists for people as God intended them to be. That is to say, as Christ—the parable of God and the paradigm of humanity in Schillebeeckx's phrase—intended them to be.

And what, finally, is this God like? Who is this supernatural personal force, this ground of our being, who calls us forth from nothingness into a divine destiny? God may well be, as the theologians report, ultimately simple. But the descriptions of God are legion and complex. Some of the most telling of these, I submit, are those biblical images that speak directly to the heart and experience. For example:

> God is called . . .
>
> "our refuge and strength" in Psalm 46 NRSV
>
> "the God of all consolation" in 2 Cor 3 NRSV
>
> "the God of steadfastness and encouragement" in Rom 15:5 NRSV
>
> the one on whom we should "cast all anxiety" in 1 Pet 5:7 NRSV

In truly worshipping such a God, we are also at whatever age in life, invariably transformed ourselves. We are invited by this same God to know the inscrutable and surpassing transcendent mercy from within, at its very heart. If we age well, the child re-emerges in us. We grow freer, lighter—sharing the lifeblood of the One who is the eternal now, present to us moment to moment, as the Timeless is to time.

As we attain the youth that can only come with aging faithfully, we return to the simple carol of our Christmases past: *venite adoremus*—come, let us adore.

> When time would beat us down, and leave us cheerless or desperate . . .   Venite Adoremus.
>
> When we would grow bored and cynical about life and all that we cannot in our limitations comprehend . . .
>   Venite Adoremus.
>
> When we would try to seize life on our terms alone and cast it in our own image . . .   Venite Adoremus.
>
> When we would lose our perspective and wit, taking ourselves too seriously . . .   Venite Adoremus.
>
> When we would falter or fall, giving in to lukewarmness and mediocrity . . .   Venite Adoremus.

Thus do our lives find at last their true center. Thus do the small rills of our lives enter wider pulsing streams. Thus do we cross bridges that link us to mainlands more infinite in their expanse than we could ask or imagine. And thus do our hearts find the haven where they are finally and truly their own, precisely because they belong so intimately and intricately to others . . . and to that Divine Other who beckons us unrelentingly to life to the full.

TO LIFT UP HEARTS
The Jerusalems of Our Lives

Since the 1980s in particular, Americans have had their consciences troubled by the plight of the growing number of those who are homeless and impoverished in the midst of an affluent culture. It is a tragic and jarring sight, especially in our major urban areas. And yet, the nation has an additional phenomenon of homelessness to torture the moral imagination: the uprootedness and loss of a sense of home-base among those who are economically secure, comfortable, and well-domiciled.

America today is a nation in which the number of citizens living alone has increased over three-fold in one generation. In many cases, of course, this represents definite choice, and a good healthy choice at that. But such a style of living can carry with it the threat of isolation and disconnection. Additionally, divorce now ends nearly one-half of all marriages in this country. And while the painful divorce process may represent at times tragic necessity, it also so often leaves in its wake deep wounds of family instability and broken hearts and homes.

Not surprisingly, then, *home,* the place traditionally associated with rootedness, increasingly appeals to sensitive people as a "haven in a heartless world," to borrow a phrase from social commentator Christopher Lasch. Home, not so much as a mere geographical category, but as a privileged place of memory and imagination; challenge and comfort; acceptance and belonging. Home as the last-ditch preserve of nurture, wit, tenderness, clean slates, and new beginnings.

Our literature, our films, our popular music are shot through with the longing for home. One of the first great classics of Western literature, *The Odyssey*, is all about old Ulysses trying to get *home*. Augustine, on the first page of his *Confessions*, talks about the restlessness of the human heart until it finds that elusive center. Frost and Eliot often turn to the image of home—and by no means in a sentimental sense—as their organizing poetic images.

Nor does the tug of this commanding image fail to dominate the world of American sport. That American comic sage George Carlin has observed: "In football, the object is to march into enemy territory and cross his goal. Baseball is played on an ever-widening field with boundaries that reach to eternity. [In baseball] the object is *to go home*."

In life, as in baseball, going home isn't always easy to accomplish. In a very real sense, once one attains the much-coveted place, the journey has only just begun. For home represents, in a wonderful paradox, the dynamic as well as the settled. It can be a place of identity, support, growth, and transformation. And yet all good things can be badly used. Homes, too, have their ambiguities and contradictions. They can be broken; can become centers of mediocrity and vegetation; of intimidation and even violence. It's not enough that we go home. We need to go to the right home. And we need to go home right.

But once we do find a home, an emotional and spiritual center, what Merton once called in another context "true north" on the compass, then we become true pilgrims, and not just wanderers on the planet Earth. We become creatures of both roots and reach. We become free of our terrible burdens of constant attempts at producing self-meaning, self-justification, and self-happiness.

One useful guide I have found in the search for a life-giving home base comes from the recent work of a psychologist with a fine spiritual touch, Michael Cavanagh. In his book titled *Make Your Tomorrow Better*, Cavanagh explores the inner geography of the human heart, mapping out its genuine needs, and charting the disasters that can occur when false emotional nurture—psychological junk food—is ingested in the attempt to assuage what are genuine and healthy hungers.

In particular, Cavanagh notes that parallel to humanity's basic physical needs are primal emotional longings crucial to human health. The four major forces driving us from within, he delineates as the needs for security, acceptance, achievement, and self-transcendence.

In reaching for these realities, the developing person can discover the inner mystery, the crucial balance point, that we have been identifying as *home*. The evocation of home awakens in the biblical believer strong emotional echoes. In the 84th Psalm, the writer insists that those who have accepted the invitation to make the house of God their own home, and thus come to their true identities at last, carry that home with them wherever they go.

It is as if they have been to Jerusalem, and now take something of Jerusalem to every place that they may be. Everywhere they turn, they find the Jerusalems of their lives. When they traverse the bitter valley, they bring with them light, hope, nurture, and kindliness. As St. Francis of Assisi intuited in the thirteenth century, where they do not find light, they bring light; in bringing light to others, they may discover it within themselves.

If ever there were days in which it is salutary to bring light to the earth, these are the days. In this century, now nearing its conclusion, a century that has long been aflirt with darkness, we may just find the mettle to show, as Auden once wrote, "an affirming flame." And in the process, we may find that we can respond with fuller hearts to the old invitation in the Latin preface of the Mass: *Sursum Corda*—to lift up our hearts.

TO GO HOME
TO THE KINGDOM
The Fond Ambush of God

It is unreliably reported that George Bernard Shaw once sent a pair of opening night tickets to one of his new plays to a man he didn't particularly like: one Winston Spencer Churchill. There was, of course, a note attached. It read: "Bring a friend, if you have one."

Churchill, full of mock gallantry, returned the tickets with regrets, noting that he was already engaged for the opening night. Of course there was more. A request: "May I have tickets for the second performance . . . if *you* have one?"

In suggesting that Churchill was passing friendless through the world, Shaw had cut to the quick. "Every man passes his life in the search after friendship," the American sage Emerson had written. And in assessing the pistons that drive a human life, Freud had argued that love and labor are paramount. If we search our own experience, we find that little is more important to us in life than the connection to wider worlds that comes our way through friendship and work.

The great saints and sinners of history have felt keenly these awesome drives that haunt and hallow us. And so have the more ordinary mortals like ourselves who seek and find, then stumble and search again. These twin drives deep within us consume the

81

greater part of our energies. They tease and seduce us; they coax and demand.

Love and labor are like the arms of God in the world. They embrace us, even as we embrace them in return. Through them we are invited into the divine creativity, each in our own modest, but unique way. In each we will discover, by turns, exhilaration and exasperation, sunlit vistas and dark nights of the soul.

If they are to be effective, these arms must enfold, but never desperately clasp or smother. The great religions of the world, especially those of the West, Judaism, Christianity, and Islam, join in these insistences:

> It is only when we stop trying desperately to force reality, other people, and our own lives into the tight molds that *we* have insisted upon . . .

> It is only when, in the words of Karl Rahner, we stop trying to be our own sufficiency and rip from the earth more than it was meant to give . . .

> It is only *then* that we begin to sense the realities that God renews constantly within us:

> The poise.
> The grace.
> The courage . . . to go forward in life.

> To strain
>   for excellence
>   for fullness
>   for justice
>   for humor and happiness.

Such a struggle and search will teach us patience and courage as well. For we will inevitably discover stings and contradiction, frustration and failures along the way. We must wander forth from our inner selves, and at times return again. This endless dynamic is known to all the great spiritualities of the world as the cycle of *kenosis-plerosis*—emptying out and coming again to a new and greater fullness. In entering into this process of mystery and pain, we discover the only truths about ourselves and our world and our God worth knowing. Until we proceed with full heart along that endless journey, we will be like listeners to some metaphysical radio station sending forth a clear channel AM signal, while we relentlessly stay on the FM band.

The great figures of the Western faiths have often set out on just such perilous journeys: Abraham, Moses, Muhammad—even Jesus himself, the traveling preacher. So often they bid us to have resolve as we go on our way. "Do not let your hearts be troubled," Jesus had pointedly and poignantly told the disciples in the Last Supper discourse as recorded in John's Gospel. We may irreverently wonder if these sojourners of faith would be so sanguine if they lived in our world, watched our nightly news, read our daily papers.

The simple fact is that they have been in our tangle. They know it from the inside. They have known "the horror . . . the horror" that Joseph Conrad reported so terrifyingly in *The Heart of Darkness*. They have been inside chaos. And it has been inside of them. But they have seen and sensed and been grasped by something more.

That something more involves the re-casting of our vision, both without and within. Not of exotic forces that are distant, spooky, and shapeless. Rather of presences that prove themselves to be noble, true, good, brave, and persistent. We, too, get unmistakable glimpses of such realities in the people, places, and situations that make up our days . . . if we know how to see and hear, touch and feel, beyond the masks of the ordinary.

Jesus had a name for that realm in which we might learn to see and hear with a new intensity. He called it the kingdom:

> The kingdom that finds us even as we seek it.
>
> The kingdom in which the friendships and goals of our labors at last flourish and signify.
>
> The kingdom that makes our consciences our guides, as Disraeli put it, and not just our accomplices.
>
> The kingdom that lets us come home and become ourselves at last.

To conclude with another British story just as hard to document as the one with which we began: Robert Louis Stevenson was once asked for a comment on the death of poet Matthew

Arnold. "Poor Matt," he said. "He is undoubtedly in heaven. But I bet he doesn't like God."

If we go forth to take on the two great tasks of attaining worthy friendships and tasks in life. If we go well-educated and well-resolved, then we will find God neither a stranger nor one we don't like.

Rather, God will be there in the tangle and complexity that shakes us even as it steadies us; that stings as it heals; that mingles life and death in the cosmic dance of being.

We can in an ultimate sense put by our worry; can live a life without cosmic care . . . only when we have found the God of the kingdom to be the kindly Mystery who awaits us, in Emily Dickinsons's awesome phrase, in "fond ambush." That Mystery is our gracious Source who empowers us, and then allows us to form our own personality, create our own face with which to meet the face and fuller embrace of God.

That is the God who summons us relentlessly . . . in friendship and labor, in weal and woe,

> to befriend
> to excel
> to speak out our own names at last, loud and true.

Section Three
PRAYERS:
MATINS AND VESPERS

PRAYER FOR MATINS
Morning

Gracious God, I render offering of myself with all that this day holds as yet unseen from me: joys and sufferings, hopes and diminishments.

I offer myself as bread and wine are offered, symbols of our fragile lives, signs that show forth the fibers of our work and the joys of our celebration. As I join myself to the Eucharistic sacrifices given this day, transform me into your body and blood in this place and this time for the doing of your will, in which alone I find my peace.

Let me find refuge today in *faith,* that strengthening perspective of deeper vision that enables me to see beyond the obvious, the here and now; that childlike approach to life that allows me to trust in your presence. Let me know that you steady me and love me clean through, even when my situation makes no sense to my limited vision. Help me to see with eyes of penetrating faith that you are everywhere as absolutely and entirely as if you were nowhere else.

Let me find refuge today in *hope,* the virtue that can find, under your grace, creativity in the face of the seemingly absurd, and opportunity even in adversity. If I stumble around in dry or barren valleys, help me to make of them a place of springs and refreshment for others, thus finding my only true drink. May I bring to the places of shadow points of light; and to climes that are frigid, the warmth that comes from closeness to your patient heart. Like Jesus, may I go around doing good.

Let me find refuge today in *love,* not in vague sentiment, but in a courageous befriending of this time and place to which you have committed me. Let me become healer and helper to those in need, those I see and those I do not. Let me love justice and be its agent today. May I thus be saved as I seek to serve, clinging to you alone, finding my strength to love from your energies let loose on the earth.

Help me to be calm today. To expect the unexpected. To be at rest even as I work. To let go the false securities of my supposed self as I long for the true self that you call me, by name, to be. Help me to value process more than things that I produce. Lead me not so much to want all things for myself as to be sharing of all things for your sake. Suffer me not the disillusionment of trying to force my way and my expectations on all things.

Glory be to the Father who creates me; the Son who brings me back from the lures of futility; the Holy Spirit who sanctifies me and makes me whole, a union of myriad parts. Blessed be the Holy and Undivided Trinity now and forever. May Mary, in her loving fidelity, be truly my advocate and my mother. May I, like her, revel with my whole being in God my Savior. May I long to see the Living God face-to-face in the community of all creatures.

May my coming to you, in that vast company be my final destiny. May it be the morning star that bids me enter this day fullhearted. Resolved to be in truth: faithful; free; compassionate; just; and in all things joyful. Thus may I be a sacred heart in the world today. For you are my friend, my hope, my challenger, my comforter. World without end.

Amen.

PRAYER FOR VESPERS
Evening

The day draws down, Holy One, and evening calls us to itself. The approaching darkness speaks to us in many ways if we but listen:

> It speaks to us of a hush and stillness, the putting aside of a day's tasks, satisfactions, and cares.

> It bids us let go of the energies of the day that we have sought to channel to the doing of your will.

> It reminds us that we can stand aside from the awful stress of taking all meanings and directions upon our narrow selves, turning from our intensities to rest in the intimacy of your inexhaustible and loving self.

Night reminds us too of the good and evil that mingle on our troubled planet earth, and the ways in which we have contributed to each this day. Hear, Lord, our prayer of repentance for our turnings from your way to our own. Heal and calm us. Grant us new courage and heart for this evening and its morrow.

Again, let us kindle the little lights that are our own; and that turn our inner eyes to you as source of light unfailing. The candles we light have more right to exist than all the darkness.

Help us be reassured that throughout this day there has been, in this world's turmoil, a divine caress. Let those waters that have swirled around us cleanse but not engulf. May we be mindful of our baptism, a plunging into your suffering and death; yet, over-all, a pledge of the resurrection to which you have called us.

We remember in the darkness the inevitability of death for each and all. Even at our birth it does but stand aside a bit and at each turn of the earth calls us closer to itself. This, too, is part of our destiny, a step in life, a passage to reality in its fuller dimension. Help us always to be ready for the coachman of our mortality, whenever he should call. May we be transported at last to the in-ner immensities of your being, now veiled from our mortal sight.

Drive from our hearts fear, loneliness, and any bitter malice. Help us to see ourselves aright. Deepen our vision. Lighten our hearts. Let us be more truly yours, and we will most assuredly be-come more fully ourselves, in the untold vastness of the commu-nity of the faithful ones.

Now you may dismiss your servant in peace. Gentle God, we have seen glimpses of your salvation. Those glimpses give us heart and hope and bid us rest in you in trusting simplicity, as a child in its mother's arms. We take refuge this night in the tenderness of your heart, just as we have sought energy this day in the tough-ness of your call.

Encircled by Mary, our most gracious advocate, all the angels and saints, and all holy creatures as our companions, we rest in your presence and your promise. May all things be well, for all crea-tures in weal and woe. This night and all nights until eternity.

Amen.